Staying Together "Discovering God's purpose for your Marriage"

Loretha Tate

All scripture references and quotations, as marked AMP & AMPC, are taken from the Amplified Bible Classic Edition of the Bible (public domain), unless otherwise stated.

Written by Loretha Tate

T2 Counseling Services
1820 The Exchange STE 400
Atlanta, G 30339

DEDICATION

I DEDICATE THIS BOOK TO MY LOVING HUSBAND FOR THE INSPIRATION AND THE SUPPORT HE'S PROVIDED ME IN WRITING THIS BOOK.

MOST OF ALL MY MOM, LUCILLE BROWN "RIH". THANKS FOR SETTING THE EXAMPLE OF HOW TO BE A WOMAN OF GOD AND STAYING TOGETHER BY GOD'S GRACE AND MERCY.

Staying Together

Table of Contents

T2 Counseling Services

"Talk2Tate"

ACKNOWLEDGMENTS

I GIVE HONOR TO GOD, FOR ALLOWING ME TO WRITE THIS BOOK. I THANK MY HUSBAND, CHILDREN AND GRANDCHILDREN. I WANT TO THANK MY PASTOR, APOSTLE DONALD JOHNSON FOR SPEAKING THIS BOOK INTO EXISTENCE. MY PRAYER IS YOU DISCOVER WHO YOU ARE IN CHRIST AND THE DIVINE PURPOSE OF YOUR MARRIAGE.

CHAPTER ONE

MARRIAGE is generally understood as the union of a man and woman for cohabitation and procreation. It goes beyond a man and a woman living together and deciding to have children. Marriage is beyond that. It is a lifetime commitment to another; it is a lifetime of trust, a lifetime of forgiveness, a lifetime of love, a lifetime of wholeness, a lifetime of conversation, and a lifetime of purpose. Marriage was instituted and ordained by God for companionship, as could be seen after God created Adam; He saw it was not good for the man to be alone, so He made him a helpmeet. God created Eve for Adam not to be lonely, so he could have somebody to talk to, and to partner with him. Marriage is also an avenue for discovery. Both men and women discover their identity in God. God's description of love is a description of His own character. This is why He made a helpmeet for the man. This is an act of love. He does not want the man to live in loneliness.

He wanted the man to enjoy the benefit of companionship. He made him a companion, a burden bearer; His true purpose for them is to live a life of happiness.

I was hanging out at a tavern on a Saturday night, sitting at the bar. During this time, I began to think about my life, how I had been lonely for quite a while now. Almost all my friends had been married, and I began to wonder what could have been wrong. I had previously been in a relationship; however, it did not work out. Not because he was not good enough for me or that I was not good enough for him. We just had different perspectives on how our relationship should be. Yes, true, I was raised up in a Christian home. I knew the dos and don'ts of what a godly relationship should be, but we both wanted something different. His perspective was quite different from mine. He wanted more than I could offer, and I was not ready to prevent or to alter the purpose of God in my life. Since then, I haven't been in any real relationship, and it had just been me.

I was brought back to reality from my thought by a gentle touch from a gentle-looking man. I hardly could say anything. I was startled, and I realized there were thoughts in my heart of being single. I heaved a deep sigh, and I looked at the man standing right there, next to me.

Hello, he said. I apologize if I startled you, you really look familiar to me. Never mind, I said. It was a prompt startling to bring me back out of the core of my thoughts. You can take a seat, I said to him. He gracefully sat down and introduced himself. My name is Derrick, and you are? Loretha, I said. Wow! I have met you before I would never forget a beautiful name and a beautiful woman like you. I grinned and faked a smile and thanked him for the compliment. It had been a minute since I heard such a compliment from a man, particularly after the breakup from my previous relationship. Yes, – Cordiree? We nodded in agreement and laughed intensely. We continued to converse until I was leaving the tavern, and I gave my number to him reluctantly, however, I was hoping to see and hear from him again.

Just about some weeks later, we bumped into each other again at the same venue. And this time, our conversation was a little more detailed than the first. We talked about our jobs and what we do for a living. Derrick is such a hilarious man and was fun to be with. For the two times we had talked, he was not boring. He did most of the talking while I did the smiling, laughing, and grinning.

Tick.... tock... tick.... tock .... The clock was ticking fast, and we both had to leave and head home. We both left with the notion of wanting to do this more often, this time not in a tavern setting.

The next morning, I got a call from Derrick that he enjoyed the time that we spent together that evening, and he wanted to see me again. He hoped we could see each other before the weekend was out. I was excited about the thought of us hanging out, and this only meant another way to be out of my thoughts of everyday life issues and having someone to listen to. We agreed to see each other on Sunday evening.

The night went so fast that before the twinkling of an eye, it was Sunday evening already. I did all I had to do on time so we could meet. After church, I went home to relax and freshen up before we met. Derrick and l had picked out a modest restaurant for us to meet. I got to the restaurant at exactly six, but by the time I got there, Derrick was already there waiting for me. I apologized for keeping him waiting. As a gentleman, he smiled, stood up, and pulled out the chair for me to sit, then he said it was better for him to have to wait as opposed to me waiting on him. Besides, you are right on time. I was the one who came earlier. I smiled, but behind my smile, I marveled at his gentlemanliness.

I was a bit more concerned about our meeting together more than I should have been. The reason behind this was bleak to me. It was, after all, the first time we would be spending time together not as couples in a relationship, but as two strangers who became friends and are on the journey of knowing each other. We ordered our food for the evening and had a great evening.

It is hard and difficult to leave someone you care about and love. This is because you have put all of your energy into it and have envisioned a future together. It makes you so emotional and leaves an imprint on your heart. This could have just been a way of God saving you from a wounded heart in marriage. It is okay to be hurt in a relationship. It places you at a better place of knowing God more and discovering your essence for living. It also allows you to discover what God has for you as His child. I overcame the hurt, fright, emotions, and allowed myself in on the journey of knowing God intimately. I was well into this when Derrick came along in my life.

Derrick and l decided to take the friendship a little deeper. So, as friends, we began seeing each other more often than it was initially. We had more times together with dates, dinners, and events. It was all through adventurous, fun, and wonderful moments.

CHAPTER TWO

I had finished my under graduate education at age 22. I was more of the listener and providing insight into friendships rather than the life of the party kind of girl. I believe this made me more of a reserved and discerning type of young woman. I studied the people around me before making friends, let alone opening up to them about the things I was dealing with. Such also, was my attitude when Derrick came onto the scene. I love listening to him while he talked rather than me talking or contributing to the discussion. Well, talking had not been my thing; however, Derrick was very good at this. He initiates a conversation and tries as much to carry me along and for me to contribute to the discussion. I'll only tease him about going on ahead while I listened. He is such rhetoric.

As the years went by, we traveled on adventures; we teased each other and talked about our funny experiences in life. Derrick would surprise me with gifts at moments I least expected. We called each other more often and regularly. I began opening up to him. The feelings were mutual. Neither of us felt we wanted to be far from each other, and the climax of it was when Derrick proposed to me. He decided to put a ring on it. We were so elated by the years we had been together and had so many fun times. However, as believers, we did not take the time to seek God's face before delving into the big part of life. We did not know God's plan, His purpose and mindset towards us both as regards to us being married. We did not seek Him to find out if we would be compatible as one.

As a young lady who was still knowing God and discovering my purpose, I was reassured and felt that Derrick had an important role to play in my life, along with the fulfillment of my destiny. I just wasn't sure how.

It is easy to get a person to be a life partner, but it is much more difficult to be partners for life. Venturing into marriage without consideration could be catastrophic. Just like anyone who wants to start a business or invest in any business or organization will have to research before venturing into the business word. Marriage is exactly just like that. We don't have to delve into marriage without proper findings, discoveries, and considerations.

Love is a common language everyone speaks, and it is so casually used that it is so common that one does not know what it is to love. Some have the feeling of lust and call it the feeling of love.

Many use the word 'love' deceitfully, but despite all the improper use of the word 'love' and the mistaken belief we all still yearn and long for true love. You can only find true love in God, and this is the Agape kind of love. This is because it is unexplainable. Love can only be found in God- 'for God so Love'- 1John 3:16; 1John 4:8. When we Love God and are soaked in His love, it will not be difficult to love others, even our spouses. Love helps us through any circumstance in our marital life.

When trials come, and things don't go the way we want and expect. Why does it put us through? This is because 'there is no fear in love, but perfect love casts out fear because fear hath torment. He that feareth is not made perfect in love.

The perfect definition of love is found in 1 Corinthians 13:4-8...

Love is not arrogant or rude. Love does not insist on its own way. Love endures long and is patient and kind; love is never envious nor boils over with jealousy, and is not boastful of vein glory. Love does not display itself haughtily. It is not conceited- arrogant and inflated with pride; it is not rude- unmannerly and does not act unbecomingly. Love (God's Love in us) does not insist on its own rights or its own way, for it is not self-seeking. It is not touchy or fretful or resentful, and it takes no account of the evil done to it (it pays no attention to a suffered wrong).

It does not rejoice at injustice and unrighteousness but rejoices when right and truth prevail. Love bears up under anything, and everything that comes is ever ready to believe the best of every person, its hopes are fadeless under all circumstances, and it endures everything (without weakening). Love never fails (never fades out or becomes obsolete or comes to an end). As for prophecy (the gift of interpreting the divine will and purpose), it will be fulfilled and pass away; as for tongues, they will be destroyed and cease; as for knowledge, it will pass away (it will lose its value and be superseded by truth).

True love is about total submission. It is a total self-giving and a lifetime of devotion to one another. Total self-giving is living a life of absolute commitment to each other. You live your life as a wife for your husband, and you live your life as a husband for your wife. Just like Colossians 3:18-19 says, 'Wives submit yourselves unto your husbands as it is fit in the Lord. Husbands love your wives and do not be bitter against them".

There is a saying that another man's food is another man's poison. This talks about the human personality. No two people like the same thing. The same is applicable in marriage. The husband and the wife become one as two individuals with different personalities. The truth is their personalities may not be compatible. The attitude one expects from the person you will be spending your entire life with may be totally the opposite of what you see or experience in the early years of your relationship, just as in my case. However, over time, you will begin to blend.

There is always something more to be expected. Marriage is full of its own surprises and challenges. It is not always sweet. Sometimes, there are moments of regret, hate, sorrow, love, surprises, anger, and annoyance, but whatever the case is, spouses, thrive on overcoming.

CHAPTER THREE

In our relationship, my husband had always been the one who initiated our in-depth conversation and bringing up conversations for me to complete them. This was at a period of my life when I was unclear about my identity. So, I always found it to be as though he was intentionally hurting me, intentionally trying to be difficult and that he was against me.

Communication is also very important in relationships, homes, and marriages. It is the key to every successful relationship. If there is no communication, it is a sign of a much deeper problem, and there is no sign of external behavior to lessen the severity that will work. Marital problems can be traced back to either of the partners not responding well in communication, or there is a communication bridge between the couples. Communication problems have to do with how either of the partners focuses on listening to each other. Communication between couples should be deliberate and intentional. Couples should schedule a time for serious discussions, and this should be beyond the surface level of just saying 'Good morning,' 'welcome back honey,' 'how are you doing today?' No! It should not be a shallow conversation you must go deeper.

Fynn Lowery, the writer of 'Covenant Marriage,' says, 'Communication is the lifeblood of a marriage.'

According to Gary Chapman, in a survey concerning why marriages failed, he said that about 86% of marriages that failed is because of lack in communication.

One aspect of communication is verbally affirming your spouse for the good things he or she does. A Psychologist, William James, stated that the deepest principle in human nature is the craving to be appreciated.

The bible also emphasized this: Proverbs 12:25- 'Anxiety in a man's heart weighs it down, but an encouraging word makes it glad.' Good words are encouraging. It shows you value and appreciate each other. Then, when this is lacking, anxiety is the atmosphere that feels the home. Proverbs 16:24- 'Pleasant words are as a honeycomb, sweet to the mind and healing to the body.' Words are very important. Good words were spoken to soothe the body. Ephesians 4:29; 1 Thessalonians 5:11.

Sometimes, rather than appreciating our spouses, we sometimes criticize rather than compliment forgetting that death and life are in the power of the tongue. It is the same mouth used in praising that is also used for cursing; an act that should not be. James 3:10. It is established that evil words destroy Proverbs 11:29, and harsh words stir up anger.

When there are unwholesome words in the house, it could create or cause challenges between spouses. If this is the case, it is possible to triumph over it. You can improve at complimenting each other by:

- Praying to seek God for help.
- Set a goal to complement your spouses every day.
- Practice self-control.
- Learn to control your anger.
- Look for your spouse's strength and praise when due rather than focusing on the weaknesses and finding faults.
- Ensure to compliment, even in the presence of others.

God's desire is for you to have a successful marriage. As husbands and wives, if you love yourselves, then one thing you should be doing is talking.

CHAPTER FOUR

When you cannot talk about the problems or challenges you are encountering in your relationship, then it becomes grievous. The inability to talk about them puts your relationship, home, and marriage in serious trouble. Communication is described as a way of sharing either nonverbal or verbal information with another person in a manner that can be understood. Before there can be any effective communication, there must be talking, listening, hearing, and understanding. The most significant of the list is understanding. Sometimes, a message can be passed across without it being understood. So, for a message to actualize the purpose to which it is said or sent, it must be well understood. Ensure that whatever it is you are sending or saying is not too ambiguous or vague. Many times, it is even possible to say something and mean the opposite of what you are saying. To have a good understanding, one needs to pay close attention, and this can be achieved by being attentive and concentrating fully with your entire being to the discussion.

Couples communicate all of the time they spend together, and even when they are apart. Here are a few statistics: communication is 7%, body language is 55%, and what verbal is 38%. The tone of our voice distorts the flow of the message sent and could infer another meaning to what we say. It is also very essential to study and know your spouse's way of communication. What your spouse does not respond to is also a form of communication. It is called the silent form of communication. The bad aspect of this communication is wrong messages are passed because there is no one- way rule to understand the non-verbal messages. The way it is understood is dependent on who receives the message. Real communication requires verbalization. In verbal communication, we pass across our feelings, likes, and dislikes ideas and concerns through voicing it out.

It is not just possible to leave what you want to say in your mind and expect your partner to read your mind.

In a good and successful relationship, partners talk about everything openly, transparently, and spontaneously. Nothing is held back so as not to give room for manipulations. The moment communication ceases, the relationship begins to fade away. Ensure that in your communication, there is no obstruction or hindrance. When there is communication gap, the couples become disabled like a person suffering from stroke, and if they do not make a conscious effort to resuscitate your communication tact, the relationship may die, and the relationship might not be redeemable again.

It looks easy to COMMUNICATE with each other, and we just do it. When holding a conversation, you should be fully in touch with what is going on. In this chapter, we would consider the book of Solomon as an illustration as to why communication is very important and how communication should be in homes, relationships, and marriages.

Among the multitudes who read the Bible, there are comparatively few who have a clear understanding of the Song of Solomon. Some have thought it to be a collection of songs, but it is more generally understood to be a sort of drama, and the positive interpretation of which is impossible because the identity of the speakers and the length of the speeches are not disclosed.

The Song of Songs [the most excellent of them all], which is Solomon's. 'Let him kiss me with the kisses of his mouth! [She cries. Then, realizing that Solomon has arrived and has heard her speech, she turns to him and adds] For your love is better than wine! [And she continues] The odor of your ointments is fragrant; your name is like perfume poured out. Therefore, do the maidens love you!

Draw to me! We will run after you! The king brings me into his apartments! We will be glad and rejoice with you! We will recall [when we were favored with] your love, more fragrant than wine. The upright [are not offended at your choice, but sincerely] love you. I am so black, but [you are] lovely and pleasant [the ladies assured her]. O you daughters of Jerusalem, [I am as dark] as the tents of [the Bedouin tribe] Cedar, like the [beautiful] curtains of Solomon! [Please] do not look at me, [she said, for] I am swarthy. [I have worked out] in the sun, and it has left its mark upon me.

My stepbrothers were angry with me, and they made me the keeper of the vineyards, but my own vineyard [my complexion] I have not kept. [Addressing her shepherd, she said] Tell me, O you whom my soul loves, where you pasture your flock, where you make it lie down at noon. For why should I [as I think of you] be as a veiled one straying beside the flocks of your companions? If you do not know [where your lover is], O you fairest among women, run along, follow the tracks of the flock, and [amuse yourself by] pasturing your kids beside the shepherds' tents. O my love [he said as he saw her], you remind me of my [favorite] mare in the chariot spans of Pharaoh.

Our cheeks are comely with ornaments, your neck with strings of jewels. We will make for you chains and ornaments of gold, studded with silver. While the king sits at his table [she said], my spikenard [my absent lover] sends forth [his] fragrance [over me]. My beloved [shepherd] is to me like a [scent] bag of myrrh that lies in my bosom. My beloved [shepherd] is to me a cluster of henna flowers in the vineyards of En-Gedi [famed for its fragrant shrubs].

He brought me to the banqueting house, and his banner over me was love [for love waved as a protecting and comforting banner over my head when I was near him].

Sustain me with raisins; refresh me with apples, for I am sick with love. [I can feel] his left hand under my head and his right-hand embraces me! [He said] I charge you, O you daughters of Jerusalem, by the gazelles or by the hinds of the field [which are free to follow their own instincts] that you not try to stir up or awaken [my] love until it pleases.

[Vividly, she pictured it] The voice of my beloved [shepherd]! Behold, he comes, leaping upon the mountains, bounding over the hills.

My beloved is like a gazelle or a young hart. Behold, he stands behind the wall of our house, and he looks in through the windows, he glances through the lattice.

My beloved speaks and says to me, Rise, my love, my fair one, and come away. For, behold, the winter is past; the rain is over and gone. The flowers appear on the earth; the time of the singing [of birds] has come, and the voice of the turtledove is heard in our land.

The fig tree puts forth and ripens her green figs, and the vines are in blossom and give forth their fragrance. Arise, my love, my fair one, and come away. [So I went with him, and when we were climbing the rocky steps up the hillside, my beloved shepherd said to me] O my dove, [while you are here] in the seclusion of the clefts in the solid rock, in the sheltered and secret place of the cliff, let me see your face, let me hear your voice; for your voice is sweet, and your face is lovely. My heart was touched, and I fervently sang him my desire] Take for us the foxes, the little foxes that spoil the vineyards [of our love], for our vineyards are in blossom. [She said distinctly] My beloved is mine and I am his! He pastures his flocks among the lilies.

Then, longingly addressing her absent shepherd, she cried] Until the day breaks and the shadows flee away, return hastily, O my beloved, and be like a gazelle or a young hart as you cover the mountains which separate us. In the night, I dreamed that I sought the one whom I love. [She said] I looked for him but could not find him.'

What can be noticed in the above excerpt? It is a dialogue between two lovers. Not only is it a dialogue, but it is conversational. There is a reply from each of them for all that was discussed. A dialogue can only be conversational when there is genuine love between two people. Amos chapter three, verse three, says, 'Can two come together except they are agreed?' There is a relationship of affection between the bridegroom and his espoused bride. The choice of words was affectionately declaring openly the in-depth of their love for each other. Is your discussion, dialogue with each other conversational? Are you careful about your choice of words? Are your words seasoned and sweet to the hearing of your spouse? If it does not, there is no other option than for you to carefully choose your words. Be conversational in your communication.

Further illustrations will be more persuasive.

'[She said] I am only a little rose or autumn crocus of the Plain of Sharon or a [humble] lily of the valleys [that grows in deep and difficult places]. But Solomon replied, Like the lily among thorns, so are you, my love, among the daughters. Like an apple tree among the trees of the wood, so is my beloved [shepherd] among the sons [cried the girl]! Under his shadow, I delighted to sit, and his fruit was sweet to my taste. He brought me to the banqueting house, and his banner over me was love [for love waved as a protecting and comforting banner over my head when I was near him]. Sustain me with raisins, refresh me with apples, for I am sick with love. I can feel his left hand under my head, and his righthand embraces me! [He said] I charge you, O you daughters of Jerusalem, by the gazelles or by the hinds of the field [which are free to follow their own instincts] that you not try to stir up or awaken [my] love until it pleases. [Vividly, she pictured it] The voice of my beloved [shepherd]! Behold, he comes, leaping upon the mountains, bounding over the hills. My beloved is like a gazelle or a young hart. Behold, he stands behind the wall of our house, and he looks in through the windows, he glances through the lattice. My beloved speaks and says to me, Rise up, my love, my fair one, and come away. For, behold, the winter is past; the rain is over and gone. The flowers appear on the earth; the time of the singing [of birds] has come, and the voice of the turtledove is heard in our land. The fig tree puts forth and ripens her green figs, and the vines are in blossom and give forth their fragrance. Arise, my love, my fair one, and come away. [So I went with him, and when we were climbing the rocky steps up the hillside, my beloved shepherd said to me] O my dove, [while you are here] in the seclusion of the clefts in the solid rock, in the sheltered and secret place of the cliff, let me see your face, let me hear your voice; for your voice is sweet, and your face is lovely. [My heart was touched, and I fervently sang him my desire] Take for us the foxes, the little foxes that spoil the vineyards [of our love], for our vineyards are in blossom. [She said distinctly] My beloved is mine and I am his! He pastures his flocks among the lilies. [Then, longingly addressing her absent shepherd, she cried] Until the day breaks and the shadows flee away, return hastily, O my beloved, and be like a gazelle or a young hart as you cover the mountains [which separate us].'

The bridegroom singled out his bride from among other women. He compared his bride to the lily in the garden while other women he compared to thorns in the garden. A lily is a beautiful flower; thorns are ugly and can painful when it pierces you. The garden is the world. This illustrates that when you get involved with other women asides from your wife, you get poisoned. Only let the beauty of your spouse captivate you. Do not be carried away by others. They are just siding attractions. Don't just get soaked in it. Proverbs 7: 1-: 'My son, keep my words; lay up within you my commandments for use when needed and treasure them. Keep my commandments and live and keep my law and teaching as the apple of your eye. Bind them on the tablet of your heart. Say to skillful and godly Wisdom, you are my sister and regard understanding and insight as your intimate friend that they may keep you from the loose (strange) woman from the adventures who flatters with and make smooth her words... in the twilight, in the evening; night black and dense was falling over the young man's life. And behold, there met him a woman, dressed as a harlot and sly and cunning of heart. She is turbulent and willful; her feet stay not in her house; now, in the streets, now in the marketplaces, she sets her ambush at every corner. So, she caught him and kissed him, and with impudent face she said to him, sacrifices of peace offerings were due from me; this day I paid my vows. So, I came forth to meet you that you might share with me the feast from my offering; diligently, I sought your face, and I have found you. I have spread my couch with rugs and cushions of tapestry, with striped sheets of fine linen of Egypt. I have perfumed my bed with myrrh, aloes, and cinnamon. Come, let us make fill of love until morning; let us console and delight ourselves with love... with much justifying and enticing arguments, she persuades him, with the allurements of her lips she leads him to overcome his conscience and his fears and forces him along. Suddenly he yields and follows her reluctantly like an ox moving to the slaughter, like one in fetters going to the correction to be given to a fool or like a dog enticed by food to the muzzle. Till a dart of passion pierces and inflames his vitals, then like a bird fluttering straight into the net he hastens, not knowing that it will cost him his life. Listen to me, therefore, o you sons, and be attentive to the words of my mouth. Let not your heart incline towards her ways; do not stray into her paths. For she has cast down many wounded; indeed, all her slain are a mighty host. Her house is the way to sheol, going down to the chambers of death.'

Lilies are special; they cannot just be found anywhere. Thorns are found almost everywhere. Often, they are found along paths, on the field even in the midst of flower garden. There is nothing beautiful about thorns except pain and damnation. Anyone who treads through the thorny path ends in destruction. She uses enticing words. Her enticing words are filled with deception, and once you fall prey and a victim, your end will be that of destruction, damnation, and death.

There is a way that seems right unto a man, but the end thereof are the ways of death. Proverbs 16:25. There is no alternative with God- when He instructs or commands, He wants prompt and complete obedience. The Holy Scripture states that if we are obedient, then we shall receive goodness from the Lord. So, if you want to receive goodness from the Lord and to eat the fruit of your marriage, stay in the path of godliness.

'In the night, I dreamed that I sought the one whom I love. [She said] I looked for him but could not find him. So, I decided to go out into the city, into the streets and broad ways [which are so confusing to a country girl] and seek him whom my soul loves. I sought him, but I could not find him. The watchmen who go about the city found me, to whom I said, have you seen him whom my soul loves? I had gone but a little way past them when I found him whom my soul loves. I held him and would not let him go until I had brought him into my mother's house, and into the chamber of her who conceived me. I adjure you, O daughters of Jerusalem, by the gazelles or by the hinds of the field that you stir not up nor awaken love until it pleases. Who or what is this [she asked] that comes gliding out of the wilderness like stately pillars of smoke perfumed with myrrh, frankincense, and all the fragrant powders of the merchant? [Someone answered] Behold, it is the traveling litter (the bridal car) of Solomon. Sixty mighty men are around it, of the mighty men of Israel. They all handle the sword and are expert in war; every man has his sword upon his thigh, that fear be not excited in the night. King Solomon made himself a car or a palanquin from the [cedar] wood of Lebanon. He made its posts of silver, its back of gold, its seat of purple, the inside of it lovingly and intricately wrought in needlework by the daughters of Jerusalem. Go forth, O you daughters of Zion, and gaze upon King Solomon wearing the crown with which his mother [Bathsheba] crowned him on the day of his wedding, on the day of his gladness of heart. '

Even when the couples are miles apart, their soul yearns for each other. When one is in distress, the other's mind is not at rest until everything is okay and sorted with the spouse.

'How fair you are, my love [he said], how very fair! Your eyes behind your veil [remind me] of those of a dove; your hair [makes me think of the black, wavy fleece] of a flock of [the Arabian] goats which one sees trailing down Mount Gilead [beyond the Jordan on the frontiers of the desert]. Your teeth are like a flock of shorn ewes that have come up from the washing, of which all are in pairs, and none is missing among them. Your lips are like a thread of scarlet, and your mouth is lovely. Your cheeks are like halves of a pomegranate behind your veil. Your neck is like the tower of David, built for an arsenal, whereon a thousand bucklers, all of them shields of warriors hang. Your two breasts are like two fawns, like twins of a gazelle that feed among the lilies.

Until the day breaks and the shadows flee away, [in my thoughts] I will get to the mountain of myrrh and the hill of frankincense [to him whom my soul adores]. [He exclaimed] O my love, how beautiful you are! There is no flaw in you! Come away with me from Lebanon, my [promised] bride, come with me from Lebanon. Depart from the top of Amana, from the peak of Senir and Hermon, from the lions' dens, from the mountains of the leopards. You have ravished my heart and given me courage, my sister, my [promised] bride; you have ravished my heart and given me courage with one look from your eyes, with one jewel of your necklace. How beautiful is your love, my sister, my [promised] bride! How much better is your love than wine! And the fragrance of your ointments than all spices! Your lips, O my [promised] bride, drop honey as the honeycomb; honey and milk are under your tongue. And the odor of your garments is like the odor of Lebanon. A garden enclosed and barred is my sister, my [promised] bride — a spring shut up, a fountain sealed. Your shoots are an orchard of pomegranates or a paradise with precious fruits, henna with spikenard plants, Spikenard, and saffron, calamus, and cinnamon, with all trees of frankincense, myrrh, and aloes, with all the chief spices. You are a fountain [springing up] in a garden, a well of living waters, and flowing streams from Lebanon. [You have called me a garden, she said] Oh, I pray that the [cold] north wind and the [soft] south wind may blow upon my garden that its spices may flow out [in abundance for you in whom my soul delights]. Let my beloved come into his garden and eat its choicest fruits.'

Here are complimentary praises from the spouse. Sweet words that give healing to the heart. There is nothing more attractive to a man than a woman who has dignity and pride in who she is, so also does the woman. The deeper feelings of passion and trust are a pleasant result of the daily choices to love each other.

'I have come into my garden, my sister, my [promised] bride; I have gathered my myrrh with my balsam and spice [from your sweet words, I have gathered the richest perfumes and spices]. I have eaten my honeycomb with my honey; I have drunk my wine with my milk. Eat, O friends [feast on, O revelers of the palace; you can never make my lover disloyal to me]! Drink, yes, drink abundantly of love, O precious one [for now I know you are mine, irrevocably mine! With his confident words still thrilling her heart, through the lattice, she saw her shepherd turn away and disappear into the night].

I went to sleep, but my heart stayed awake. [I dreamed that I heard] the voice of my beloved as he knocked [at the door of my mother's cottage]. Open to me, my sister, my love, my dove, my spotless one [he said], for I am wet with the [heavy] night dew; my hair is covered with it. [But weary from a day in the vineyards, I had already sought my rest] I had put off my garment—how could I [again] put it on? I had washed my feet — how could I [again] soil them? My beloved put in his hand by the hole of the door, and my heart was moved for him. I rose up to open for my beloved, and my hands dripped with myrrh and my fingers with liquid [sweet-scented] myrrh, [which he had left] upon the handles of the bolt. I opened for my beloved, but my beloved had turned away and withdrawn himself, and was gone! My soul went forth [to him] when he spoke, but it failed me [and now he was gone]! I sought him, but I could not find him; I called him, but he gave me no answer. The watchmen who go about the city found me. They struck me, and they wounded me; the keepers of the walls took my veil and my mantle from me. I charge you, O daughters of Jerusalem, if you find my beloved, that you tell him that I am sick from love [simply sick to be with him]. What is your beloved more than another beloved, O you fairest among women [taunted the ladies]? What is your beloved more than another?

beloved, that you should give us such a charge? [She said] My beloved is fair and ruddy, the chief among ten thousand! His head is [as precious as] the finest gold; his locks are curly and bushy and black as a raven. His eyes are like doves beside the water brooks, bathed in milk and fitly set. His cheeks are like a bed of spices or balsam, like banks of sweet herbs yielding fragrance. His lips are like bloodred anemones or lilies distilling liquid [sweet scented] myrrh. His hands are like rods of gold set with [nails of] beryl or topaz. His body is a figure of bright ivory overlaid with [veins of] sapphires. His legs are as strong and steady pillars of marble set upon bases of fine gold. His appearance is like Lebanon, excellent, stately, and majestic as the cedars. His voice and speech are exceedingly sweet; yes, he is altogether lovely [the whole of him delights and is precious]. This is my beloved, and this is my friend, O daughters of Jerusalem!'

Do you often long for one another? Are you able to sleep, and yet your heart is awake for your partner if they are out on a business trip? When your hearts are joined in such a way that it constantly and continually pounds for the other *nearby.*

'How fair you are, my love [he said], how very fair! Your eyes behind your veil [remind me] of those of a dove; your hair [makes me think of the black, wavy fleece] of a flock of [the Arabian] goats which one sees trailing down Mount Gilead [beyond the Jordan on the frontiers of the desert]. Your teeth are like a flock of shorn ewes that have come up from the washing, of which all are in pairs, and none is missing among them. Your lips are like a thread of scarlet, and your mouth is lovely. Your cheeks are like halves of a pomegranate behind your veil. Your neck is like the tower of David, built for an arsenal, whereon a thousand bucklers, all of them shields of warriors hang. Your two breasts are like two fawns, like twins of a gazelle that feed among the lilies.

Until the day breaks and the shadows flee away, [in my thoughts] I will get to the mountain of myrrh and the hill of frankincense [to him whom my soul adores]. [He exclaimed] O my love, how beautiful you are! There is no flaw in you! Come away with me from Lebanon, my [promised] bride, come with me from Lebanon. Depart from the top of Amana, from the peak of Senir and Hermon, from the lions' dens, from the mountains of the leopards. You have ravished my heart and given me courage, my sister, my [promised] bride; you have ravished my heart and given me courage with one look from your eyes, with one jewel of your necklace. How beautiful is your love, my sister, my [promised] bride! How much better is your love than wine! And the fragrance of your ointments than all spices! Your lips, O my [promised] bride, drop honey as the honeycomb; honey and milk are under your tongue. And the odor of your garments is like the odor of Lebanon. A garden enclosed and barred is my sister, my [promised] bride— a spring shut up, a fountain sealed. Your shoots are an orchard of pomegranates or a paradise with precious fruits, henna with spikenard plants, Spikenard, and saffron, calamus, and cinnamon, with all trees of frankincense, myrrh, and aloes, with all the chief spices. You are a fountain [springing up] in a garden, a well of living waters, and flowing streams from Lebanon. [You have called me a garden, she said] Oh, I pray that the [cold] north wind and the [soft] south wind may blow upon my garden that its spices may flow out [in abundance for you in whom my soul delights]. Let my beloved come into his garden and eat its choicest fruits.'

The spouse appraises the beauty of the bride. He commends her beauty. Several expressions show the spouse delights in her. The bride also ascribes all she has as the affluence of her spouse's grace. He also professes his love and affection towards her while, in return, she delights in him. These words are not just mere flattering words but a sincere admiration of how they value each other. They both would not even mind doing so amid others. Do you just flatter your spouse? Are your appraisals sincere? Are they not just mere words just to suit the present moment? Think about this if you truly want to stay together with each other.

'I have come into my garden, my sister, my [promised] bride; I have gathered my myrrh with my balsam and spice [from your sweet words, I have gathered the richest perfumes and spices]. I have eaten my honeycomb with my honey; I have drunk my wine with my milk. Eat, O friends [feast on, O revelers of the palace; you can never make my lover disloyal to me]! Drink, yes, drink abundantly of love, O precious one [for now I know you are mine, irrevocably mine! With his confident words still thrilling her heart, through the lattice, she saw her shepherd turn away and disappear into the night]. I went to sleep, but my heart stayed awake. [I dreamed that I heard] the voice of my beloved as he knocked [at the door of my mother's cottage]. Open to me, my sister, my love, my dove, my spotless one [he said], for I am wet with the [heavy] night dew; my hair is covered with it. [But weary from a day in the vineyards, I had already sought my rest]

I had put off my garment—how could I [again] put it on? I had washed my feet—how could I [again] soil them? My beloved put in his hand by the hole of the door, and my heart was moved for him. I rose up to open for my beloved, and my hands dripped with myrrh and my fingers with liquid [sweet-scented] myrrh, [which he had left] upon the handles of the bolt. I opened for my beloved, but my beloved had turned away and withdrawn himself, and was gone! My soul went forth [to him] when he spoke, but it failed me [and now he was gone]! I sought him, but I could not find him; I called him, but he gave me no answer. The watchmen who go about the city found me. They struck me, and they wounded me; the keepers of the walls took my veil and my mantle from me. I charge you, O daughters of Jerusalem, if you find my beloved, that you tell him that I am sick from love [simply sick to be with him]. What is your beloved more than another beloved, O you fairest among women [taunted the ladies]? What is your beloved more than another?

beloved, that you should give us such a charge? [She said] My beloved is fair and ruddy, the chief among ten thousand! His head is [as precious as] the finest gold; his locks are curly and bushy and black as a raven. His eyes are like doves beside the water brooks, bathed in milk and fitly set. His cheeks are like a bed of spices or balsam, like banks of sweet herbs yielding fragrance. His lips are like bloodred anemones or lilies distilling liquid [sweet scented] myrrh. His hands are like rods of gold set with [nails of] beryl or topaz. His body is a figure of bright ivory overlaid with [veins of] sapphires. His legs are as strong and steady pillars of marble set upon bases of fine gold.

His appearance is like Lebanon, excellent, stately, and majestic as the cedars. His voice and speech are exceedingly sweet; yes, he is altogether lovely [the whole of him delights and is precious]. This is my beloved, and this is my friend, O daughters of Jerusalem!'

Communication is not just in conversation and dialogue. It is actually more than that. It had been discussed earlier that communication should be deliberate, intentional, and in depth. Sexual intimacy is also an act of communication. This is because there is a mutual understanding between spouses.

'*Let my beloved come into my garden*,' that is an invitation. How often do you respond to your partner's sexual needs? When you feel the urge for intimacy, do not reject your partner just because you are not in the mood? Do you satisfy your partner? Do you just come together only for the benefit of procreation? Your relationship is not just for the benefit of procreation. Sex makes you more intimate with yourselves.

It is an act of love. It shows how well you value yourselves. Let your communication be intimate. It gives you the freedom to be free with one another and to get to know yourselves better.

'Where has your beloved gone, O you fairest among women? [Again, the ladies showed their interest in the remarkable person whom the Shulammite had championed with such unstinted praise; they too wanted to know him, they insisted.] Where is your beloved hiding himself? For we would seek him with you. [She replied] My beloved has gone down to his garden, to the beds of spices, to feed in the gardens and to gather lilies. I am my beloved's [garden], and my beloved is mine! He feeds among the lilies [which grow there]. [He said] You are as beautiful as Tirzah, my love, and as comely as Jerusalem, [but you are] as terrible as a bannered host! Turn away your [flashing] eyes from me, for they have overcome me! Your hair is like a flock of goats trailing down from Mount Gilead. Your teeth are like a flock of ewes coming from their washing, of which all are in pairs, and not one of them is missing. Your cheeks are like halves of a pomegranate behind your veil. There are sixty queens and eighty concubines, and virgins without number; but my dove, my undefiled and perfect one, stands alone [above them all]; she is the only one of her mothers, she is the choice one of her who bore her. The daughters saw her and called her blessed and happy, yes, the queens and the concubines, and they praised her. [The ladies asked] Who is this that looks forth like the dawn, fair as the moon, clear and pure as the sun, and terrible as a bannered host?[The Shulammite replied] I went down into the nut orchard [one day] to look at the green plants of the valley, to see whether the grapevine had budded and the pomegranates were in flower. Before I was aware [of what was happening], my desire [to roam about] had brought me into the area of the princes of my people [the king's retinue]. [I began to flee, but they called to me] Return, return, O Shulammite; return, return, that we may look upon you! [I replied] What is there for you to see in the [poor little] Shulammite? [And they answered] As upon a dance before two armies or a dance of Mahanaim.

The people around know she is the fairest of women. This is because of the way the bridegroom esteemed his bride. How do you both portray each other? Do you esteem one another even in the presence of the people around you? If you undervalue your spouse, those around you will just simply do that as well. Remember, Proverbs 31, her husband is known in the city's gate... and her husband sings her praise.

Then her companions began noticing and commenting on the attractiveness of her person] How beautiful are your feet in sandals, O queenly maiden! Your rounded limbs are like jeweled chains, the work of a master hand. Your body is like a round goblet in which no mixed wine is wanting. Your abdomen is like a heap of wheat set about with lilies. Your two breasts are like two fawns, the twins of a gazelle. Your neck is like a tower of ivory, your eyes like the pools of Heshbon by the gate of Bath-rabbim. Your nose is like the tower of Lebanon which looks toward Damascus. Your head crowns you like Mount Carmel and the hair of your head like purple. [Then seeing the king watching the girl in absorbed admiration, the speaker added] The king is held captive by its tresses. [The king came forward, saying] How fair and how pleasant you are, O love, with your delights! Your stature is like that of a palm tree, and your bosom like its clusters [of dates, declared the king]. I resolve that I will climb the palm tree; I will grasp its branches. Let your breasts be like clusters of the grapevine, and the scent of your breath like apples and your kisses like the best wine— [then the Shulammite interrupted] that goes down smoothly and sweetly for my beloved [shepherd, kisses] gliding over his lips while he sleeps! [She proudly said] I am my beloved's, and his desire is toward me! [She said] Come, my beloved! Let us go forth into the field; let us lodge in the villages. Let us go out early to the vineyards and see whether the vines have budded, whether the grape blossoms have opened, and whether the pomegranates are in bloom. There I will give you my love. The mandrakes give forth fragrance, and over our doors are all manner of choice fruits, new and old, which I have laid up for you, O my beloved!'

Mutual endearment should always be there between spouses. Even when there are distractions here and there, be focused on making your home peaceful. Interruptions will come from different people, even from those you highly esteem. Do not talk down, but rather, make your partner precious in their sight. When you do this, the desired respect will be inevitable. Always admire every part, and every aspect of your spouse.

Looking forward to the shepherd's arrival, the eager girl pictures their meeting and says] Oh, that you were like my brother, who nursed from the breasts of my mother! If I found you without, I would kiss you, yes, and none would despise me [for it]. I would lead you and bring you into the house of my mother, who would instruct me. I would cause you to drink spiced wine and of the juice of my pomegranates. [Then musingly she added] Oh, that his left hand was under my head and that his right hand embraced me! I adjure you, O daughters of Jerusalem, that you never [again attempt to] stir up or awaken love until it pleases. Who is this who comes up from the wilderness leaning upon her beloved? [And as they sighted the home of her childhood, the bride said] Under the apple tree I awakened you; there your mother gave you birth, where she was in travail and bore you. Set me like a seal upon your heart, like a seal upon your arm; for love is as strong as death, jealousy is as hard and cruel as Sheol (the place of the dead). Its flashes are flashes of fire, a most vehement flame [the very flame of the Lord]! Water cannot quench love; neither can floods drown it. If a man offered all the goods of his house for love, he would be utterly scorned and despised. [Gathered with her family and the wedding guests in her mother's cottage, the bride said to her stepbrothers, when I was a little girl, you said] We have a little sister, and she has no breasts. What shall we do for our sister on the day when she is spoken for in marriage? If she is a wall [discreet and womanly], we will build upon her a turret [a dowry] of silver; but if she is a door [bold and flirtatious], we will enclose her with boards of cedar. [Well] I am a wall [with battlements], and my breasts are like the towers of it. Then was I in [the king's] eyes as one [to bq2e respected and to be allowed] to find peace. Solomon had a vineyard at Baal-Hamon; he let out the vineyard to keepers; everyone was to bring him a thousand pieces of silver for its fruit. You, O Solomon, can have your thousand [pieces of silver], and those who tend the fruit of it two hundred, but my vineyard, which is mine [with all its radiant joy], is before me! O you who dwell in the gardens, your companions have been listening to your voice—now cause me to hear it. [Joyfully the radiant bride turned to him, the one altogether lovely, the chief among ten thousand to her soul, and with unconcealed eagerness to begin her life of sweet companionship with him, she answered] Make haste, my beloved, and come quickly, like a gazelle or a young hart [and take me to our waiting home] upon the mountains of spices!'

The affection between the bridegroom and his bride is very strong, so, therefore, in order to live and stay together, the affection between spouses should be strong. Work at making your relationship alive and strong. Ensure that you fellowship together both physically and spiritually. Do not let anyone interrupt and interfere in your home. Lift yourselves up in the place of prayer and Godly counsel. Always be in constant intimacy with one another.

When my husband-initiated conversations, I took him to be irritating and that he was against me. I had to go back to the originator of marriage to figure who I was. I knew Him to be the one to help me commit myself to my husband. My temperament being an introvert, was not going to save my marriage. I decided to rule over my temperament and not my temperament ruling me. I decided to let myself begin to open up to him, being involved in his conversation and not to see it as a way of him being difficult or being against me. I had to try to understand him better. I began reading and studying the word of God. I began to pray more and sought counseling. I had to learn my identity in Christ so I could truly love my husband and be the wife he needed and the wife I desired to be to him. I made the ultimate decision to go back to college to become a counselor. I believed it would be a way to help me in my marriage and likewise be able to help others who might need a breakthrough in their marriages.

I enrolled at a Christian University, and through my journey to a master's degree in Professional Counseling, I began knowing more about God. I read and studied the Bible more often; I engaged in exercising my spiritual muscles; I read several books on relationships, marriages, and creating a happy home. In the quest to know more of God, I discovered the following, and it gladdens my heart to share it with you:

There's a difference between knowing about God and being in relationship with God. Seeking after Jesus is different from seeking Jesus. Those who seek Jesus look for him for what they can get from him. John 6, Mary Magdalene, sought Jesus. You can know about someone without knowing the person. Just as an American is to America, so also is a Christian to Christ. Paul, because of his exceeding knowledge, desires a much greater relationship with God.

There's something in you that desires a relationship with God. Philippians 3:10 says 'For my determined purpose is that I may know Him, that I may progressively become more deeply and acquainted with Him, perceiving and recognizing and understanding the wonders of His Person deeper and more clearly, that I may in that same way come to know the power outflowing from His resurrection which He exerts over believers. And that I may so share His sufferings as to continually transform in Spirit into His likeness even to His death in the hope.

When you are making a choice to marry, it should not be based only on romantic feelings. Romance should not take the place of love. Just because a guy is romantic by giving gifts, surprising you with so many things should not overwhelm you. I am not saying being romantic is bad. All I am saying is that you do not base your relationship on how romantic someone is with all he or she does. Being romantic does not tell you anything about the character because it could be mistaken for true love. Just like it has been said earlier, marriage requires diligence and efforts.

CHAPTER FIVE

MARRIAGE is the reflection of God's covenant with us. You just don't enter into a marriage relationship today, and the next, you opt-out. Dr. Samuel Adams and Ben Young wrote: 'There are lots of decisions we make in life that are bad and could be wrong, but later, we recover from them. Like selecting a wrong car but can later trade it for another after some time. We could make the wrong choice of University or College, but at the end of the day, get a transfer to another. You can take the wrong job, but later find yourself another job you like more. You can make foolish financial decisions and even end up in debt, but you recover by getting wiser and paying off the debts. All these decisions may carry some adverse consequences that are incomparable to the marriage relationship because you can easily opt-out of them and find another alternative. However, in marriage, there is no alternative. You just have to learn to love and learn to stay together. The relationship becomes better not by trying to change your partner but by learning how to focus on improving yourself. Love actually is not staying together, and it is living together.

At a certain point in our relationship, there was a breach. It certainly was a dark period for us both. A certain lady was striving to get close to Derrick. She started as being friends with him. This period was the time I was still reserved, and I had just started my master's degree in Professional Counseling. She, of course, had her time devoted to Derrick. He finally got someone he could have a conversation with. Something I lacked at the time. They would talk and discuss so many topics and things. Gradually, I began seeing Derrick drift away from me. I tried so much to control the situation, but it seemed as though I was nagging – yes, nagging. I began complaining, and at every step I took, I became more and more upset. The more upset I got; I became bitter; but remember that bitterness leads to strife.

What was wrong? I could not take it any longer. I would not just sit back and watch another woman with my man. You may ask... but Derrick has not done anything wrong. He is just friends with her and nothing more. Well, can I tell you there is something more to it. Just friends? But that is how it starts. I decided to open my eyes and not allow the devil in my home... no, not even a foothold. The Bible says in 1 Peter 5:8 'Be well balanced (temperate, and sober in mind), be vigilant and cautious at all times; for that enemy of yours, the devil, roams around like a lion roaring in fierce hunger, seeking someone to seize upon and devour.' I decided in my heart to withstand the devil in faith by not letting any strange woman sway Derrick away. I also purposed in my heart to make my home a safe and peaceful place by working on myself and being a partner to my spouse. It takes two to partner together. I also came to realize that the love that sustains a marriage is not something we wish for but something we work at. So, therefore, couples who want to keep the love they have for each other to ensure a joyful life need to actualize that communication, trust and conflict resolution is important and must ensure that they share common values.

Through the period of my counseling training, I learned about the confident woman and who she is. I studied and researched so well about the confident woman to help me through the journey of my relationship. Here are my thoughts on who the confident woman is.

She is not fearful: A woman who is confident does not live in abject fear. She refuses to live in fear. 2 Timothy 1:7 says, 'For God did not give us a spirit of timidity (of cowardice, of craven and cringing and fawning fear), but He has given us a spirit of power and of love and of calm and of well-balanced mind and discipline and self-control.' This plainly reveals to us that fear is not from God, but it is of the devil. A tool the devil uses to deprive us of enjoying our lives. Fear causes a person to run and to shrink back in life. Hebrews 10:38 says, 'but the just shall live by faith, and if he draws back and shrinks in fear, my soul has no delight or pleasure in him.' We are not to draw back in fear but to live by faith.

She takes actions: A confident woman has no other choice than to constantly take deliberate actions on overcoming the challenges of life, especially those that may arise to destroy her future and home.

She is positive: When a woman is full of confidence, she is positive. She is very optimistic. Being optimistic is much more beneficial and fruitful than being negative.

She overcomes trying situations: A person only becomes a failure when he or she quits trying.

Do not give up on life when life has not yet given up on you. So, when difficult times come, do not get drenched in it. Learn to be an overcomer and strive to soar above them. To have a good home and relationship, all depends on the woman.

Staying Together

57

CHAPTER SIX

Not only should the woman be confident in herself, but she must also exude the quality of the woman revealed in Proverbs 31: 10 – 31 'A capable, intelligent woman, who is he who can find her/ she is far more precious than jewels and her value is far above rubies or pearls. The heart of her husband trusts in her confidently and relies on and believes in her securely so that he has no lack of [honest] gain or need of [dishonest] spoil. She comforts, encourages, and does him only good as long as there is life within her. She seeks out wool and flax and works with willing hands [to develop it]. She is like the merchant ships loaded with foodstuffs; she brings her household's food from afar [country]. She rises while it is yet night and gets [spiritual] food for her household and assigns her maids their tasks. She considers a [new] field before she herself with strength [spiritual, mental, and physical fitness for her God-given task] and makes her arms strong and firm. She tastes and sees that her gain from work [with and for God] is good; her lamp goes or accepts it [expanding prudently and not courting negligence of her present duties by assuming other duties]; with her savings [of time and strength] she plants fruitful vines in her vineyard. She girds not out, but it burns on continually through the night [of trouble, privation, or sorrow, warning away fear, doubt, and distrust]. She lays her hands to the spindle, and her hands hold the distaff. She opens her hand to the poor; yes, she reaches out her filled hands to the needy [whether in body, mind, or spirit]. She fears not the snow for her family, for all her household are doubly clothed in scarlet. She makes for herself coverlets, cushions, and rugs of tapestry. Her clothing is of linen, pure and fine, and of purple [such as that of which the clothing of the priests and the hallowed cloths of the temple were made]. Her husband is known in the [city's] gates when he sits among the elders of the land. She makes fine linen garments and leads others to buy them; she delivers to the merchant's girdles [or sashes that free one up for service]. Strength and dignity are her clothing, and her position is strong and secure; she rejoices over the future [the latter day or time to come, knowing that she and her family are in readiness for it]! She opens her mouth in skillful and godly Wisdom, and on her tongue is the law of kindness [giving counsel and instruction]. She looks well to how things go in her household, and the bread of idleness (gossip, discontent, and self-pity) she will not eat. Her children rise up and call her blessed (happy, fortunate, and to be envied); and her husband boasts of and praises her, [saying], Many daughters have done virtuously, nobly, and well [with the strength of character that is steadfast in goodness], but you excel them all. Charm and grace are deceptive, and beauty is vain [because it is not lasting], but a woman who reverently and worshipfully fears the Lord, she shall be praised! Give her of the fruit of her hands and let her own works praise her in the gates [of the city] '

In support of the verses written above, there are other scriptural passages that reveal the power a woman has in making her home to work. Yes! True, the man also has his own part to play, but the woman has more work in her hand to do in ensuring her home is successful, fruitful, and peaceful.

Proverbs 12:4 'A virtuous and worthy wife- earnest and strong in character is a crowning joy to her husband, but she who makes him ashamed is as rottenness in his bones.' If the home is to be joyful always, be a crowning joy to your husband. Be of good character and earnestly steadfast.

Proverbs 19:14 'Houses and riches are the inheritance from fathers, but a wise, understanding and a prudent wife is from the Lord.'

From Proverbs 31:10-31, being virtuous is to have an excellent moral character of admirable quality. The worth of a virtuous woman is priceless.

'A woman of noble character is hard to find, and when found, she is to be valued far above pearls and rubies.' As a woman who desires to sustain her relationship and her home, are you of noble character? Are you virtuous? Is your worth and quality admirable? Can your spouse rely on you? Does his heart trust in you? Do you comfort and encourage your husband or nag him and complain all day long? This is essential in sustaining relationships, marriages, and homes, as many marriages and homes could be saved from divorces. Are you lazy? – A lazy woman cannot sustain her home as men cannot put up with lazy attitudes. Do you procrastinate? Rather than being lazy or a procrastinator, why not decide to be zealous and build your home just as you want it to be.

Also, as a woman who desires to uphold her home, you must fight off self-doubt. James 1:6-8 says, '...only it must be in faith that he asks with no wavering, i.e., no hesitating, no doubting. For the one who wavers is like the billowing surge out at sea that is blown hither and thither and tossed by the wind. For truly, let not such a person imagine that he will receive anything he asks from the Lord, for being as he is a man of two minds- hesitating, dubious, irresolute, he is unstable and unreliable and uncertain about everything he thinks, feels and decides.' God does not answer the prayer of a double-minded person. A double-minded person is such a one that wavers in faith. Being double-minded is self-doubt, which is fear. God only responds to our faith. This is because faith is the substance of the things we hope for and the evidence of the things we have not seen.

In staying together with your spouse, have faith in the things you hope for in your relationship and home. Let your faith eyes launch into the unseen to call forth the things that be not as though they were. The things you desire in your home, relationship, and marriage that is not there, your desires and expectations that are being replaced with disappointments, pray it forth in faith.

The decision to have a happy home and to stay together in peace, love, forgiveness, honesty, commitment, and unity begins with you. Yes, it begins with you! It begins even with either of you!

You may be wondering, are the men left out of the decision in making their homes, relationships, and marriages better. No! They are not left out. They also have their parts to take in having a successful and peaceful home and staying together. Just as a relationship and home need a virtuous woman, a diligent and faithful man is also essential. Who then is the diligent and faithful man? He is such a man that performs his duty with intense concentration, focus, and responsible regard. He is such a man that is loyal, reliable worthy of trust, and engages in a sexual relationship only with his spouse.

Proverbs 20:6 'Many a man proclaims his loving-kindness and goodness, but a faithful man who can find? The righteous man walks in his integrity; blessed (happy, fortunate, and enviable) are his children after him. So, therefore, each partner should decide and make up their minds to make it work and enjoy the very best in their relationship and home.

Discover God's purpose, rely on Him, and see yourself as God sees you. You will realize that God has the very best for you from His words. Jeremiah 29:11 'For I know the thoughts and plans I have for you, says the Lord, thoughts, and plans for welfare and peace and not for evil, to give you hope in your final outcome."

Proverbs 3: 5-6 'Lean on, trust in, and be confident in the Lord with all your heart and mind and do not rely on your own insight or your understanding. In all your ways know, recognize, and acknowledge Him, and He will direct and make straight and plain your paths.' To have a successful home, you must call on God daily, trust Him for your relationship and home and know that He is able to carry you through in His hands and to give you the very best of stay. I began living in the light of this realization.

CHAPTER SEVEN

After I had finished my master's degree program, I had a counseling session with a young lady: A female manager in her mid-30s had been married to her job at the detriment of her family. It had been a tussle between her and her husband. Her career was eating deep into her family life. She had no time for her husband even though she hadn't been married for so long. She traveled a lot and had no time for her home. Along the line, her husband began seeing someone else. He started out by keeping late nights. Even at this, she wasn't so aware of her husband's new way of life until it was too late to make amends. He was in love with someone else and could not keep up with the life of his wife, not being around when he needed her. He had sought and found satisfaction and solace somewhere else. He felt fulfilled. He's got the life he wanted - so he thought.

On her return from one of her many trips, she found her home empty. Her husband was gone; he left with everything he had. The only thing he left for her was just a brown envelope. Fidgeting, she picked up the envelope from the bed, opened it only to be served divorce papers. She sobbed profusely till she drifted off to sleep. It was an unbearable sight for her as she woke up at intervals with the thought of her husband gone.

At the dawn of the next day, she awoke with the ringing of her phone. It was her husband's lawyer demanding her to make an appearance. She hurriedly dressed up and dashed through to his office. There, she met her husband with another lady, smiling radiantly.

In dismay, she tried to remember when she had seen such a wonderful smile on her husband - well, she couldn't remember. All she had seen through the years of their relationship was the complaints he had about her job. The disappointment on his face whenever she denies him in bed with the excuse of being tired from a day's work. She hadn't been a good wife; she couldn't manage her home. And now, he is happy in another woman's hands. She lost him. She didn't want him gone, but it was too late. She did not want to see herself separated from her husband. She was hesitant. She wanted another chance. She hoped her marriage could work out. And that's when she came to me for a way out of the mess, she found herself. Was she to just sign the paper and let go of her husband to another woman? We had many counseling sessions. I talked to her about her getting a re-orientation about her finding a balance with her home and work life. Your home comes first before your job. Too much attention to a job or career could be detrimental to your home life. The thought of her getting a divorce crumbled her wall and crushed her. Her confidence was shattered. But this was a wakeup call for her to reestablish her life; to be reawakened; she decides on a new life. Her husband was hell-bent on the divorce because he had gotten the other woman pregnant. She eventually signed the divorce paper. She decided to hold her life together, worked so hard for a comfortable life, and seem to have it all on the outside, however it was just a façade. Something was missing. And till she found it; a new chapter of her life began. Full of nature and love. She thought she could get it all done by herself. And then she narrates further that through one of her trips, she met a promising young gentleman who decided to date her after a few months of dating. She wanted to know more about how to do her homework for the second time so that there will not be a repeat of what had happened to her previously. She needed directions for the right path to move forward, and however, if she continued in that path all by herself, she would fall into the same routine again. All she had to do was to rely solely on God. Yes, God hates divorce, but He is also capable of healing you of the pain of it at all when you are in this situation.

From my own part, I shared my experiences with her and led her through the part of discovering her identity in God. I encouraged her to live a better life by first, not seeing her career as a priority. Not that you should not work, however, not to take the job so much to heart that it eats deep into the peace of your home. God wants us all to be in the center of His will. And obedience is the key. There's nothing else he demands of us.

Spouses should endeavor to always be there for one another regardless of the circumstances and situations around them. Ecclesiastes 4:9-11 says 'Two are better than one because they have a good [more satisfying] reward for their labor; For if they fall, the one will lift up his fellow. Woe to him who is alone when he falls and has not another to lift him up! Again, if two lie down together, then they have warmth; but how can one be warm alone?'

Never allow your spouse to ever feel alone. By doing so, you are opening the doors of your home to the enemy.

Also, bear one another's burden. Galatians 6:2-3 'Bear (endure, carry) one another's burdens and troublesome moral faults, and in this way fulfill and observe perfectly the law of Christ (the Messiah) and complete what is lacking [in your obedience to it]. For if any person thinks himself to be somebody [too important to condescend to shoulder another's load] when he is nobody [of superiority except in his own estimation], he deceives and deludes and cheats himself.'

2 Corinthians 1:4 'Who comforts (consoles and encourages) us in every trouble (calamity and affliction), so that we may also be able to comfort (console and encourage) those who are in any kind of trouble or distress, with the comfort (consolation and encouragement) with which we ourselves are comforted (consoled and encouraged) by God. For just as Christ's [own] sufferings fall to our lot [as they overflow upon His disciples, and we share and experience them] abundantly, so through Christ comfort (consolation and encouragement) is also [shared and experienced] abundantly by us.'

2 Corinthians 1:6-7 'But if we are troubled (afflicted and distressed), it is for your comfort (consolation and encouragement) and [for your] salvation; and if we are comforted (consoled and encouraged), it is for your comfort (consolation and

encouragement), which works [in you] when you patiently endure the same evils (misfortunes and calamities) that we also suffer and undergo.

And our hope for you [our joyful and confident expectation of good for you] is ever unwavering (assured and unshaken); for we know that just as you share and are partners in [our] sufferings and calamities, you also share and are partners in [our] comfort (consolation and encouragement).'

With the help of God, I was able to encourage her with the victories He had given unto me.

I talked about Christ and all he had done for me in sustaining my home and restoring my relationship. Psalm 78:2-7 'I will open my mouth in a parable (in instruction by numerous examples); I will utter dark sayings of old [that hide important truth] — Which we have heard and known, and our fathers have told us. We will not hide them from their children, but we will tell to the generation to come the praiseworthy deeds of the Lord, and His might, and the wonderful works that He has performed. For He established a testimony (an express precept) in Jacob and appointed a law in Israel, commanding our fathers that they should make [the great facts of God's dealings with Israel] known to their children, that the generation to come might know them, that the children still to be born might arise and recount them to their children, that they might set their hope in God and not forget the works of God, but might keep His commandment.'

Obedience is the outward action that arises from the inner response of faith, love, and trust in regard to God. Jesus said, 'if you love me, you will obey my commandments' - John 14:15. While we obey others, we can joyfully remember that it is God alone who is worthy of complete obedience.

Through obedience to God, we will be able to endure in our Christian lifestyle.

CHAPTER EIGHT

A relationship means nothing without loyalty; this is because the goal in marriage is not to think alike but to think together.

James 5:16 says 'Confess to one another, therefore, your faults (your slips, your false steps, your offenses, your sins) and pray [also] for one another, that you may be healed and restored [to a spiritual tone of mind and heart]. The earnest (heartfelt, continued) prayer of a righteous man makes tremendous power available [dynamic in its working].' Prayer gives rise to love; when there is love, it gives birth to praying more. When the prayer intensifies, love increases the more. When there are things displeasing in your relationship, tell it to God; speak the words of life. God's words are life and are able to turn ugly situations around to make beautiful ones.

Mark 11:24-26 'For this reason I am telling you, whatever you ask for in prayer, believe (trust and be confident) that it is granted to you, and you will [get it]. And whenever you stand praying, if you have anything against anyone, forgive him and let it drop (leave it, let it go), in order that your Father Who is in heaven may also forgive you your [own] failings and shortcomings and let them drop. But if you do not forgive, neither will your Father in heaven forgive your failings and shortcomings.' Forgiveness is the act of forgiving someone and to stop feeling angry with someone who has done something to hurt, upset, or annoy you.

Ephesians 4: 31-32 'Let all bitterness and indignation and wrath (passion, rage, bad temper) and resentment (anger, animosity) and quarreling (brawling, clamor, contention) and slander (evil-speaking, abusive or blasphemous language) be banished from you, with all malice (spite, ill will, or baseness of any kind). And become useful and helpful and kind to one another, tenderhearted (compassionate, understanding, loving-hearted), forgiving one another [readily and freely], as God in Christ forgave you.' Diverse problems will arise in marriage and in the home. You must be ready to bring them to God in prayer, and before God can answer such prayers, you must be ready to forgive and let go of all bitterness. It is only through the help of God and the power of the Holy Spirit that forgiveness will be easy. Our Lord's Prayer teaches us that God only forgives us when we forgive others of their trespasses.

Whenever there is a problem or conflict between you both, regardless of who might be at fault, in as much as it might be difficult, learn to say 'I am sorry' and 'I forgive you.' These two words are very powerful. It does go a long way than you ever could imagine. Whenever you say 'I am sorry' or 'I forgive you,' you have to mean it. Be sure that what you are saying is true and is from your heart. When you forgive, let it be absolute. Do not refer back to previous and past incidences whenever rift arises again.

When there are repentance and forgiveness, what is your attitude? It is actually not possible that in a relationship, there won't be challenges, misunderstandings and mistakes that can sever your relationship. Your ability to repent determines how the home will thrive, and your ability to forgive will sustain the home. It takes wisdom to deal with things accordingly.

Proverbs 2:10 'For skillful and godly Wisdom shall enter into your heart, and knowledge shall be pleasant to you. Discretion shall watch over you; understanding shall keep you, to deliver you from the way of evil and the evil men, and from men who speak perverse things and are a liar. Men who forsake the paths of uprightness to walk in the ways of darkness.'

Always encourage one another in the Lord. United prayer and fellowship are a source of encouragement couples should adhere to.

Acts 4:31 'And when they had prayed, the place in which they were assembled was shaken; and they were all filled with the Holy Spirit, and they continued to speak the Word of God with freedom and boldness and courage.' There is power in united prayer by spouses prayed in unity. Our greatest form of encouragement is in God and in His word.

Colossians 3:16-19 'Let the word [spoken by] Christ (the Messiah) have its home [in your hearts and minds] and dwell in you in [all its] richness, as you teach and admonish and intelligence and wisdom [in spiritual things, and as you sing] psalms and spiritual songs making melody to God with [His] grace in your hearts. And whatever you do [no matter what it is] in word or deed, do everything in the name of the Lord Jesus and in [dependence upon] His Person, giving praise to God the Father through Him. Wives, be subject to your husbands [subordinate and adapt yourselves to them], as is right and fitting and your proper duty in the Lord. Husbands, love your wives [be affectionate and sympathetic with them] and do not be harsh or bitter or resentful toward them.'

CHAPTER NINE

THREE POWERFUL STATEMENTS; THREE SIMPLE WORDS:

- ➤ I am sorry.
- ➤ I forgive you.
- ➤ I love you.

These statements go a long way in a relationship. They are not statements you say casually, you have to mean them. I have seen many people say them without actually meaning what they say; it usually does not produce the desired result. These statements are short but powerful! When you say them, it has to come from your heart. We've already seen how collision in a relationship, especially marriage, is unavoidable. Prepare your mind and accept the fact that your spouse is human and hence imperfect —well, so are you! So, when two imperfect people come together, everything cannot be a rollercoaster all the time. You will have those moments (when everything goes exactly as you want it in your relationship), yes... cherish them, but also be prepared to forgive and accept your fault and acknowledge your love for your significant other, through the bad and the ugly.

"I am sorry."

I will start with this one —"I am sorry" because I have discovered in my years of counseling that one of the major human problems is accepting fault. It is most difficult for an individual to put the blame on himself or herself. From childhood, when things go wrong, we want to blame other people for it and excuse ourselves from every fault. It becomes amplified in a relationship! Why? You might be able to shield your faults from others outside, but when you invite someone into your life, you are also inviting them to see your faults. You can't shield your faults from them; neither can they shield theirs from you. They can try to do so, but eventually, the cat always finds its way out of the bag. A simple illustration you can probably relate to is if there was this girl in school you admire, and then you found out that you were paired as roommates for the next semester. Then you discovered the not so golden part of your roommate. You now see her when she wakes up in the morning, how she smells without her deodorant, how she looks without her makeup, how irritating she can sometimes be... and the truth is she is only herself. You are the one who should reconcile with the fact that though you admire her, she is very much human. Living with someone alone will reveal a lot about them. So, when you are in a relationship, which is beyond just living together, but involves intimacy and confiding in each other, you have to become more open to each other. If only you and your spouse can accept your imperfections and work together. We play the blame game a lot... it is in the core of humanity, and it is been in existence since the beginning of time.

'And they heard the sound of the Lord God walking in the garden in the cool of the day, and Adam and his wife hid from the presence of the Lord God among the trees of the garden. But the Lord God called to Adam and said to him, where are you? He said, I heard the sound of You (walking) in the garden, and I was afraid because I was naked and I hid. And He said, who told you that you were naked? Have you eaten of the tree which I commanded you that you should not eat?' (Gen 3:8-11 AMP)

Remember it was Adam that was given the instruction, he must have passed it on to Eve, but it was Eve that was deceived. She then proceeded to deceive her husband, who could have said no and helped her see that she had been deceived. However, see how the blame game played out.

Adam: "the woman whom you gave to be with me —she gave me (fruit) from the tree to eat, and I ate."

And the Lord God said to the woman, "what is this you have done?"

Eve: "The serpent beguiled (cheated, outwitted, and deceived) me, and I ate." (Gen 3:12-13)

Everyone had someone else to blame. Adam said it was Eve, and circuitously blamed God too, since it was His idea (...the woman whom 'You' gave to be with me...) but said nothing about his own disobedience! Eve also had the devil to blame. Was she deceived truly? Yes, she was, but did she have a choice? A definite yes! The devil only planted an idea in her mind; she said yes to carry it out; she could have said no. Adam could have been of help after Eve was deceived, he could have been the pillar of strength the family needed when the devil was trying to steal their joy, but oh no... even though the original instruction was meant for him, he caved in also.

When the devil starts to try his gimmicks to disrupt our relationships, at least one person has to stay sensitive and not be ignorant of the devices of the enemy. However, if there was an issue and you are at fault, the only way to move forward is to accept it and apologize! Yes...we must learn to apologize. "I am sorry" –three simple, harmless words. Of course, it doesn't have to be the only three words you should say, but it has to be the summary of everything you say and let it come from your heart. Sometimes, it is safer to say "I am sorry" only, truly from your heart, and move on. Because people sometimes say they are sorry, only to say other things that do not suggest that they are actually sorry. Admitting that you are sorry means that when your spouse summarizes everything you have said, the fact that you are sorry should be resounding and reassuring.

"I forgive you."

Other times, we are not at fault. Usually, in a relationship, you are either in the wrong or right whenever you fallout; you can't be wrong and right at the same time. You can both be right –progress and you can both be wrong –disconnection –lack of progress. If not at fault and your spouse admits his or her wrongdoing, you should learn to forgive. As Christians, we cannot do without 'forgiveness,' we will need to trade with it as often as necessary. The story of the Christian faith is very much centered on forgiveness. Today, we are in Christ, and forgiven. This is the celebration of God's love for humanity, our faith, hope, and justification lie in this fact. This is why we should not be 'stingy' with forgiveness; we must be generous in letting go of the hurt and the past. Prepare your mind to forgive, even before you are offended. You will discover that you don't readily take offense; the way you respond to hurt will be different. This will go a long way in your marriage and your relationship with other people.

The best part is when you two have to accept your individual faults and look for a way to move forward together. As sometimes, just as you can make progress together, you can also contribute to the disengagement in your relationship. Adam and Eve could have accepted their individual faults, rather than look for someone else to put the blame on. Therefore, James admonished that we confess our individual faults to one another (this is where you both admit "I am sorry", one to another); but he further said we should also pray for one another, that we may be healed and restored to a spiritual tone of mind and heart –this is the part you let go and forgive. Many times, I like to ask, "When was the last time you prayed for your spouse?" probably if we pray more for our spouses, they will not be overcome by faults. Well, that is exactly what James is telling us! He said our earnest prayer makes tremendous power available! When we pray for our relationship and the people we love, we will see things going in the right direction. Because this is what we do in the place of prayer, we are channeling our relationship in the right direction.

Forgiving means forgetting. If you continue to refer to the incident or continue to act in response to what happened, you are yet to forgive. Forgiveness lies in letting go; there is no need to say that we have forgiven another if we will not forget the wrong and move on. Is it hard to forget? I will not say it is easy, because it is not, but see it this way: when God forgave us, old things passed away (He never reckoned with us or relate with us based on our past. Once forgiven, God will not see the failings anymore), all things became new (He opened a fresh page and started with us). Many times, when the word 'new' is used in the Bible, it usually refers to something that has never existed before; hence, you can't attach a past to it. So, when we forgive, we should realize that we are opening a new page, and we can't attach a past to that fresh start. It doesn't mean the wrongdoing, hurt, or even the emotional pain will be wiped out of our memory; it only means we choose not to attach a past to the fresh start we are initiating. When we remember the wrong, we remind ourselves that it's a fresh start. People usually say, "We are putting the past behind us and moving on." I will love to say it differently, "We are leaving the past behind, and we are moving forward." There is no way the past can follow you to wherever you are going; it has been left behind.

"I love you."

This is one of the few phrases people place a premium on in time past. This usually means that commitment must come from the heart. Today, it can mean different things.

However, as a married couple, you must understand the power of this statement. By now, you must have realized that it means commitment and selflessness. It means I love you, no matter what... I love you, in spite of it... it is staying committed to another; it is looking beyond one's self and putting the other person first. This isn't what society defines as love many times. Love does not expect something in return; it doesn't give so it can have back. It gives selflessly. It's not a trade.

We have already examined the characteristics of this love in 1 Corinthians, chapter 13. The word used is 'charity,' old English for love. There is no true charitable cause that gives to people who can return the favor; it is usually a selfless cause. This love is the agape kind of love, the kind God has for us. The Greek word 'agape' means affection, benevolence, and goodwill.

This statement is more meaningful and powerful during difficulties in a relationship. It is quite easy to say "I love you" when everything is great, and you have each other's back. But the word has more meaning when we have to love others when they are annoying, provoking, somewhat irritating, and in their 'down moments.' Then we have actually loved a person.

This is God's love —Romans 5:8 'But God shows and clearly proves His [own] love for us by the fact that while we were still sinners, Christ (the Messiah, the Anointed One) died for us.'

We don't love their frailties or wrongdoing; we only love them in spite of it. This is how our relationship becomes stronger and thrives. You will face challenges and difficulties, but your commitment and selfless openhandedness to each other will pull you through. You don't say this in your mind, and words have no effect as thoughts; you have to verbalize them. Many people make this mistake, they admit their love, but they don't verbalize it. Your thoughts are for you, and they are not useful to another person until they become words. You have to say it. You have to reassure your spouse often. Love is another currency like forgiveness; that if we should 'spend' it more often, we will spend forgiveness much less.

CHAPTER TEN

Usually, people want to separate love from commitment. They feel they are two entirely different concepts. But they are not; there cannot be commitment without love, and when the love is *agape*, there will be commitment. God is still committed to saving people and giving them hope, all over the world, today, as He was a thousand years ago. In a relationship, love is the bedrock on which commitment is found.

Commitment is a decision you consciously make concerning something (someone) you love or something important. You can decide to stay committed to a career path, a job, to studying, and so on. You can also decide to stay committed to a person or to people. Not everyone 'in love' is committed to each other, but everyone committed to each other are in love. True love will birth commitment over time. You don't become committed to something you don't love or see as important, either negative or positive.

This was why you got married in the first place; it's not because you were both in love alone; the commitment had been birthed through that love. You both logically thought it through, and you decided if you wanted to be together then you wanted to commit yourself to a life with another person.

Committing to a cause or a person will very much depend on your thinking process, your emotional maturity, needs, personality, and lifestyle. Two people committing to each other or the same cause cannot be alike in all these characteristics, probably in some of them. Hence, it has to be a joint decision and working it out. So that even when lifestyle and needs change and you become more emotionally mature, it will not impinge on your commitment but will strengthen it.

In a marriage, you will need commitment, not just at the initial stage but always, to keep you going. Things are moving faster now; people's needs, tastes, and preferences are changing with time. Commitment is staying true to a cause despite the changes and devising ways to make it healthy and strong. Commitment helps you become resilient when your relationship (marriage) goes through disappointments and downtimes. You will learn to work together through the tough times without infringing on each other's freedom.

Commitment to a long-term process −a relationship or even a project −requires a proper 'counting the cost.' Jesus said you could not set out to build a house or go to war without counting the cost; else, you can be in the middle of the whole thing, and your resources are exhausted. And there must be a set time to round up a house building project; the house has to be completed one day. No matter how long a war goes, it has to end at some point.

You can't count the cost in your marriage the same way you will for a building project or a war. Marriage is like a building you keep working on, a building up that continues. It is like the only war that never ends –a peace treaty. You don't just go ahead and make a truce; you have to count the cost also. This always lasts longer and is much more cost-effective. It doesn't mean there wouldn't be a clash of interests, but a peace treaty means the parties will not result in a war to resolve it; a diplomatic approach will rather be engaged. David fought war almost all his life, but his son, Solomon, did not have to fight any. Many think it's because David already fought all the war, so Solomon did not have to, but subsequent kings did go to war... so Solomon's wisdom wasn't just for nothing. He counted the cost; he signed peace pacts with other kings and stayed true to it to his death. He decided to fight his war in a different way, and it was much more effective.

Everything does not require a strong commitment; we can commit to certain things casually. That is, how important the thing is to determine our level of commitment. So, you are not staying committed in a marriage for a long period because it's the norm; but because it is important to you. Commitment is not enduring; you are not trying to endure that relationship at the expense of your freedom and individuality. Commitment is an 'it takes two to tango' decision in marriage. You must envisage days when a strong windstorm will blow against what you are building together, days when there will be a clash of interests; commitment is staying together in spite of and still keep your individuality and freedom.

Commitment means you are loyal to your spouse

Loyalty means staying faithful, staying true to your decision; it is being honest about the way you feel and about your needs, as well as staying committed to your partner in all of that. Loyalty has to do with openness. Infidelity in marriages do not just happen, and it usually follows a pattern. I told you how there was a disconnection between I and Derrick, and the companionship I could not offer, someone else was willing to fill in that gap from outside. It could also be the other way around; the man might be very busy that he neglects the needs of his wife, and she starts to get that attention from someone else. This is why commitment requires the signature of both parties on the loyalty document. Loyalty should be a joint decision. How does one stay loyal in a relationship or to one's partner?

- Keep an open and truthful mind about the way you feel.

People feel that loyalty means supporting your partner's needs at the expense of their own needs. Many times, this outlook on loyalty is best seen as a desire, and it is impractical in a relationship. Although, just as in a relationship built on love and selflessness, you will always put your partner's needs before yours, but never at the expense of yours! Hence, commitment, loyalty must be well communicated between partners. Commitment in a relationship starts with staying true to yourself. Be certain you are not betraying your own feelings even from the start! Once you do that, pretense starts to creep in, and eventually, you begin to compromise. Someone who cannot stay true to himself or herself cannot be committed to another.

Be faithful to yourself first! Be open about how you feel and be completely honest too. This is impossible without proper communication. This was why we had to look at the importance of communication in a relationship extensively.

We will still need to refer to this subsequently throughout this book. Having counseled different people concerning their relationships and marriages, I have discovered that you cannot establish commitment in a relationship without an open communication line. Remember, this was how you and your partner started out in the first place. None of you would have committed to the relationship in the first place if there was no proper communication of intent and purpose. You make your intent (how you feel about the other person) known –"*I want us to be together...*"

you then get a response as to how the other person feels about you also. Many feels this ends at the conception of their relationship, but no! It is more important not to close the communication line in the relationship. This is the way you can properly establish loyalty.

• Keep an open and truthful mind about everything

Let your spouse know how you feel about everything – everything within the context of your relationship or as it affects your relationship.

Very close to the first point but different. No secrets! You can be entirely honest about how you feel in a relationship, but there are other things you are keeping from your spouse. You have to be honest about your past, present, and future. This is everything about your relationship; your partner has the right to know. The issue usually is with the past before you met each other. But you have to let your partner know everything about the past that can possibly harm your relationship.

The truth is, not every information concerning our past should concern our partner but being in a relationship means we have opened ourselves up to them entirely. We cannot keep anything from them, especially the past, they can always find out about the present or future, but it is a lack of loyalty on our part if they should find out about the past before hearing it from us. The past tells the story of who we used to be if we are still the same person or we've changed, the events or truths about us that directly affect our relationship. A young man wanted to get intimate with a lady, but he doesn't want to come clean about his past, he felt it was too ugly to admit. The lady refused to commit herself to the relationship because she expects the same of him. He was opened about his wants and desires, but he doesn't want to be open about all that concerns him. Loyalty is coming completely clean... no surprises!

If you claim you are loyal to someone, then they should not be finding out for the first time, what you should have told them, from someone else or on Facebook! This has to do with both our present and future plans. Your spouse should know about these things before anyone else if he/she has a habit of telling others before telling you or letting out all the details of your plan after you've discussed it. The same yardstick applies – loyalty is two-sided! Hence, communication is vital. Sign a pact (let there be an agreement) that no one outside your relationship has a right to that information until you both decide otherwise. Give your partner a chance to adjust and act accordingly.

Never be on the lookout for mistakes; keep an open and honest mind about everything that concerns your partner, that he or she can make the right decision and make adjustments when necessary. Loyalty will only thrive through teamwork.

Commitment means you trust your partner

One of the greatest gifts of a wonderful marriage is the ability to trust your partner. Trust that she will be true to you emotionally, trust that he will be true to his words, and trust you will both stay committed to each other. This creates safety, a deeper connection, and the capacity to love. It is sad that many homes and relationships lacks trust among themselves. Our relationship must be built on trust if we want it to stay strong and lasting.

How do you know if you trust your partner? There are certain questions you need to ask yourself. We need to consider your disposition towards your partner when trust issues arise; this goes a long way to determine if your relationship has the ingredient of trust or not.

• Are you free of concern for your partner?

This is a very important question each partner should consider individually. When you have to worry about what your partner is doing or not doing, you are yet to establish your relationship on trust. Many times, it's usually a one-sided coin, but it takes two to tango.

Commitment is two-sided; it is both loyalty and trust. Loyalty is, "*I want you to be honest and open with me... about everything.*" When you have agreed on staying loyal to each other; Trust is, "*I believe in you, I am rest assured that you will be honest and open with me.*" Trust issues begin to arise when partners hide behind the cloak of, "*I am safeguarding my heart from hurt.*" This is why there's a need to communicate and agree on being loyal to each other. It shouldn't be what one is expecting of the other, and hence, he or she becomes the 'loyalty police' in the relationship. It should be teamwork, and you must trust each other's discretion to do the right thing.

To trust someone means to give them a chance. Giving them a chance to be human, give them a chance to grow, give them a chance to make some mistakes and learn from it, give them a chance to stand to their feet and move on with you... You are simply giving room for growth. That you believe your partner can get better and better. It isn't setting a goal for your partner to meet and then screaming blue murder when they miss the mark.

It is setting a goal together and moving towards it together; when one falters, the other will extend a helping hand, and they will both move forward. When you see trust in this light, you will let go of your fears and worries; you will rather enjoy some peace of mind with your partner.

- Do you still keep some things as a secret?

You don't have a private life when you are involved with someone. In marriage, a cleaving has occurred, there is a union. This means an invitation to have your private life invaded! You called for it; you must be able to give yourself to it a hundred percent. Therefore, a relationship plagued with secrets −and yes, I said 'plagued'... secrets do not look good in a relationship, it is more like a plague. That's a mild description because secrets can destroy a thriving union. It's a ticking time bomb −is devoid of trust. If you cannot trust your spouse with certain things, certain information, certain knowledge, obviously, there is a trust issue. The beauty of your relationship is your ability to confide in each other.

You should be able to talk about just anything and everything freely, without having to hold back. You can't keep secrets and live freely around your partner. You already deny yourself your freedom and individuality. You should be most free with someone you love and want to spend the rest of your life with.

Therefore, no secrets and make your intentions and feelings known also. Do not assume your partner knows what you are going through, how you feel about something; let your intentions be plain enough. Severally, feelings and needs unvoiced will lead to doing things that will make you to keep a secret. There is no freedom in keeping secrets.

Sometimes people make the excuse of, *"if I tell her, it will destroy her... if I reveal this to him, it will destroy him."* but if you don't, the end result can be much more devastating, and then, you will not be able to take it back. There are some proper ways to go about this; you can approach a counselor together; someone involved in ministry is much better because it can be delicate in handling.

You can consider speaking to your pastor, also. You can't approach just anybody; you need to approach someone you can both trust to help you establish trust in your relationship.

CHAPTER ELEVEN

One of the major issues of married couples is the tendency to either grow apart such that they end up living separate lives or to have one actively growing, while the other refuses to reinvent himself or herself. Tastes change, tastes morph and evolve as well as the people that bear them. There are things picked up on the way, and others probably just dormant hitherto in marriage, which now seeks expression through the individuals involved. Marriage, very much like life, seeks those who would be ready to learn, unlearn, and relearn.

Take a hypothetical example of an uprising gospel artist who married a modest looking wife from a small town. Keep in mind he came from a very modest background himself, he gets exposed to the international platform of ministry, a certain degree of excellence, either by choice or circumstance doesn't seem to be fitting into his wife of his youth, yet seeks those standards to be established in his own home and ministry, without adopting a manner seeking to teach over trying to impose, might find cracks beginning to appear.

It is okay to discuss ways your partner could improve or point out something they do that is bugging you. However, too much correction or negativity can make anyone feel unworthy and unloved. Many times, when we talk about being honest about how you feel, many push it overboard and do something entirely different from what was intended. They result in always correcting their partner; this can be counterproductive. The essence of being open and truthful about your feelings is to keep the communication line open and know how you both feel and not to hurt the feelings of each other. The best way to avoid this is to make known what your needs are, leave out how, where, and when your spouse should make an adjustment. Trust your partner's discretion to do the right thing.

When they ask for help, you can do so without being bossy, and when they offer help, you don't have to be sassy; everyone needs an adjustment to move forward in life. If you correct in love, then there will be no need to have another's feelings hurt. If you receive the correction truly in love, then there wouldn't be a bruised ego. There can't be growth without a change. Change many times, deal with making corrections, and adjusting. We all had to make certain adjustments in certain areas of our lives before we could move forward. We will all have to do this, reflecting once in a while to determine the next phase of adjustments. It becomes much easier when we have someone to point it out easily! Before someone outside brings it to your attention, which can be embarrassing, it is healthier to have your spouse point it out (trust me).

Growth while it may not be an exact science, can be a journal, it can be nurtured and the indifference to being deliberate about it, brings a version of it yet untamed —retrogression – this is growth in the negative curve of life. Besides spending time enjoying each other's company, experts recommend taking the time to regularly 'check-in' and 'check-up' on how each of you is doing, both in the relationship and with life in general. When we are involved with someone, their growth as an individual is as important as their growth in the relationship. It will be selfish to be particular about only what they can offer in the relationship, while we neglect to check up on how their life's dream, vision, idea, or project is coming along.

I love the way the Foursquare app is designed to work. As someone particular about communication and growth in relationships, I was fascinated by how it works. It works with locations, and the recipients sign in at landmarks within an area. Once an individual has the highest check-in, he/she has crowned the Mayor of the place on the app, and others see it and attempt to get the position. It was all fun. In the same way, spouses should constantly check-in, sign in on their partners and become the invincible and ever reigning kings / Mayors of their partner.

There must be a deliberate action on the part of both parties in a relationship to know each other. Man is a dynamic being, ever-growing, changing, and adapting to his environment and also teaching (periodically changing) it to adapt to him. As a result, the knowledge of man is ever-increasing, and each one different from the other. Though it may be said and agreed that certain broad classifications do a good job in helping us understand ourselves and others, it is really not all there is to man. There's a quote that goes like this "God is in the details "and to explain that I'd like to say though we may have similarities, both overt and covert, differences also abound.

These differences will also help couples and prevent them from falling into the familiar cycle of comparison with other families.

In as much as we all can learn from others; we must be careful to know what works and in what circumstances it does. Anybody can post a cute picture on social media with their spouses, insert a deep quote, and lead us to believe all is perfect when it isn't. We must watch not only what we copy but also how we copy. Especially in the kingdom of God, which Christ has brought us into, we must follow and carry the right spirit, the Holy Spirit of God, without whom we're helpless on earth.

For how else can our families be kept from the wrong influence which the world system so readily offers, without the person of the Holy Spirit? The Bible says we should not be conformed to the world system, but we should renew our minds —learn, unlearn, and relearn constantly.

In a case where two people have joined themselves in blissful matrimony, it is readily obvious that being two thinking beings, irrespective of numerous intersections in character and upbringing, there'll still be differences. This is pretty normal.

Like Sara Debbie Gutfreund wrote, "A growing marriage has several dimensions to its identity too. There is the romantic dimension that first drew the couple together, the friendship that becomes stronger each year, the team identity we need for parenting, and the shared activities dimension in which growing couples' hike or bike or attend a class together. Like the parts of our individual identities, the dimensions of a growing marriage strengthen and enhance each other."

Growing together is a deliberate effort, because though married and living in the same house, couples experience life differently , and even if they did go through the same experiences for every day of their lives (which is hardly feasible), they are bound to interpret and react to them differently, hence the need to consciously confluence to understand the other.

This requires accountability, and that means you must be ready to give all. That's why it's said that such a union as marriage isn't meant for immature persons. Immaturity comes in many forms, but the character is a favorite for the marital union.

We're in the age of celebrity weddings, social media hypes, and make-believe fairy tales. If we're critically scrutinize most of the romantic stories we grew up with, we'd realize that it all ends at living happily ever after.

As we grow older, we are exposed to the sham that "happily ever after" really isn't happily ever after, however it requires commitment and steadfastness. Looking at the generation of our parents and those before them, we could see the deliberate manner with which they worked out issues. They sought primarily to build and not to pull down, to sustain and heal and possibly even endure pain, but rarely gave up.

However, those standards are falling, and we're in an age where people desire intimacy without commitment, and the end of a marriage is often predicted from the beginning by persons, not necessarily doomsayers, but because they've seen so much and have become cynics.

The family is God's design and his weapon on earth. The church is made up of families and if we set our minds to what the Scriptures say in Psalms 127:1

'Except God builds the house, they labor in vain that build it: Except God keeps the city, the watchman waketh but in vain'.

We would notice an important principle therein, where God builds a house first before watching the city. This is because a city is made up of houses with families. So, God is very interested in families because once the foundation is set right and children raised properly according to the standard of God, which is Christ, the society and its attendant parastatals will have little to worry about.

If we all as a people are progressively journeying into the light and revelation of Christ, the frontiers of darkness will be pushed back. So, this is why marriages must be gotten right. Proverbs 22:28 Remove not the ancient landmark, which thy fathers have set.

We cannot seek to journey effectively and chart our course properly if we do not properly appraise, assess and appreciate where we have been, what helped the fathers to obtain the promise; Hebrews 11:40 clearly says 'God having provided some better things for us, that they without us should not be made perfect'.

The journey to perfection in marriage shouldn't be made in isolation. It's usually said that the most important decision a person can make after his salvation and discovery of purpose is the choice of a life partner. I once read of a meeting where it was told to the men in attendance that one of the surest determinants of their fulfillment in life was their spouses, the one who knows them more than anyone.

So more than most, the decision on a marriage defines a lot on this side of eternity.

Now there is the possibility that many have embarked on this journey, and the spark has been lost, and all that's left is just sharing a home, sharing a bed, but never really sharing their lives. I hope that through these words, you'll find healing for your aching souls and be able to alter the failing coordinates. One of the most important things to remember is that in any relationship within the kingdom is to be first defined by God before anything. God's word is the standard for every relationship. The most important person is God.

Ecclesiastes 4:9 'Two are better than one; because they have a good reward for their labor'.

Ecclesiastes 4:10 'For if they fall, the one will lift up his fellow: but woe to him that is alone when he falleth; for he hath not another to help him up'. 4:11 'Again, if two lie together, then they have heat: but how can one be warm alone? ' 4:12 'And if one prevails against him, two shall withstand him; and a threefold cord is not quickly broken. '

While God celebrates the union of two, it is made beautiful and given a definition in Christ. The scriptures above refer to it as a threefold cord, and many times we could make the mistake of tagging God as the third party.

God is the first party, the author of life, the one who draws men to himself and in whom we find the perfection of love. With God as the first, we're able to define our relationships with His standard. The couple makes up the other two in the threefold cord. At this point, it would be best to put things in perspective. It might make sense to say the couple brings God along in their journey, but actually, it is God who should bring them together.

Matthew 19:4-6 'And he answered and said unto them, Have ye not read, that he which made them at the beginning made them male and female, And said, For this cause shall a man leave father and mother, and shall cleave to his wife: and they twain shall be one flesh? Wherefore they are no more twain, but one flesh. What therefore God hath joined together, let not man put asunder.'

With particular emphasis on verse 6, having fulfilled the preceding, can it be said that it is a joining birthed and sustained by God, and as such, should not be tampered with? It is the most sacred of unions that can be between man and woman.

Given that, the first and most important is our identity in Christ Jesus, our knowledge of sonship and stewardship, and due appropriation of both. Many usually look for identity in marriage;

they want to discover themselves (their purpose) through their union with others. We all have our unique identity individually! For instance, you should not find your identity as the first lady because your husband is the president; it shows you are not prepared for it. Many women are pillars behind their spouses; their husbands might not be the president, but they are first ladies in their own right. As believers, we find our identity in Christ Jesus. We define who we are, our life's purpose in Him. This discovery is a personal pilgrimage. We can make the discovery together as a couple, but we do so individually.

This is important because we must always derive our sense of worth and dignity from God and not from a person or a relationship. Our love for a person must flow from our love for God, else it would be unsustainable.

CHAPTER TWELVE

Still very much on the topic of growing together, it is as important as love and commitment. As earlier stated, people change, and one must be able to grow in view of these necessary changes – changes are normal in life.

It is possible that a couple could have known and loved God at the inception of their relationships, but due to the fate of life; involving but not limited to raising kids, trying to make a living and suchlike, they both grow cold, losing touch with their center in God. Or it could be the case that they never really knew Him, or only one party did, and this makes the relationship unbalanced.

When I met Derrick, we both knew our center must be God. We were both believers, and even though we didn't involve God at the inception of our relationship, we did not continue in that mistake. I have counseled several people in different situations in their relationship. The best thing for the category of couples who haven't found God is that they both discover Him together and experience Him individually. Their relationship will find purpose and meaning.

"We're all hungry people

Feeding on things that never fill

Till we find our place in God."

• @olu bisileko (Twitter)

Nothing and no one except God will satisfy us. In all of our quests to see our fairy tales and deepest desires come true, the real cry of our souls is for God. And if we don't get this right, we'll keep expecting the impossible; mortal and fallible people loving us in all way only God can leave us unsatisfied and highly disillusioned, yet still searching, even if we claim we're not.

If only a partner finds God or from the inception, it has always been one of them; this is what I call 'a lopsided relationship.' Only a part of what should be a union is experiencing God, and the system will experience imbalance in belief, principle, and general perception of life. If you are the believing partner, then do not forget that the effectual fervent prayer of the righteous makes tremendous power available (dynamic in its working).

Your prayer for your partner will go a long way. You can trust

God to reveal Himself in very dynamic ways to your partner. Never give up; never stop believing for your spouse.

In this case, if things do not work out at least, you can walk away with no regrets.

The fun that never ends

In pieces above, we have established that God should be the beginning of a marriage relationship and that it is a union for two mature minds, willing to submit to God.

It's never late with God. God being the beginning necessarily doesn't mean you started with God as the center; it might be a decision you only later made. It means God takes the preeminence in your marriage; you make Him the center of your lives. This decision can still be very much effective after several years of other things being the center of your marriage rather than God.

I have chosen and used the word "fun" intentionally because it has almost become the norm that the service and relationship with God by believers isn't seen as something fun-filled or worth attaining. It sometimes seems like a boring necessity, which is why the widely help opinion of most people about eternity is mostly warped and inaccurate. One of the major things that make our Christian faith beautiful is our fellowship with God, constantly beholding His face, becoming like Him, and constantly being assured of His unfailing love.

When this isn't happening in a believer's daily life, true fellowship becomes inexistent and service to God, boring and lifeless. This mostly wasn't always the case. At the time of confession and believing unto salvation, there is a new life, excitement, and vigor; however, it is a continued progression in the knowledge of, Jesus Christ, that helps the relationship. We are a people that must continually journey into light, life, and love: our refusal or inability causes misery.

As I began to get to know who I was in Christ, the vigor and excitement that wasn't in my marriage started resurfacing. The vigor was first coming back to life in me as an individual, and I began to experience 'fun' and freedom. There was no room for nagging or seeing my husband as against me anymore. My husband had that freedom, and he wanted to extend the same to me in our conversations, but I only felt he was being difficult or imposing.

I didn't have the sense of the freedom he was experiencing. Don't get me wrong, I was a good Christian, but I was yet to start defining my identity in Christ. In essence, you must know who you are, be honest with yourself, remember your spouse is your partner, and things spoken are only to help not harm. Remembering you are on the same team is imperative in relationships.

It is this principle that applies to marriage. In the initial stages of meeting a new person and getting into courtship, there is perhaps an overemphasis on romantic love, which though good and desirable, isn't enough to sustain a life together.

God's love must be the standard and only balance.

Those early days are full of fun in which one can hardly spend enough time with the other, and there is always a desire to see each other again when apart, and somehow, life happens in the marriage, and they forget to keep that alive. Like I said earlier, we were all made to be pilgrims and not settlers. We must keep journeying into perfection, and this is an intentional movement. No marriage works just by wishing; it is a process which must be worked on consistently.

Life happens to everyone, and romance isn't exclusive preservation of the wealthy (which we already are in Christ). Having founded a marriage in God, it takes the grace of God to build on it. After all, as a Father, he is our source and sustainer.

Keep the communication line open always.

Proper communication will help you establish growth in your relationship. A couple that does not communicate is very prone to acting in disloyalty towards each other and growing apart. So, this point cannot be overemphasized.

Before the invention of mobile phones, couples would wait upon each other's letters. When one couple writes another, he or she will longingly wait for the reply. There was an open line of communication, and this continues into marriage –if the husband or wife had to travel elsewhere. Today, communication is much easier. We can decide if it's going to be a phone call or a video call; we can text now and get the reply in a few seconds. I feel the communication between couples should get better as the means to do so have, but no, it seems to have gotten worse. A couple can be together on their phones, texting, and they are saying nothing to themselves; but yet saying so much to other people via texts. Many relationships have trust issues because of the easy way they can now communicate with others. Whenever they call their partners, it's not to talk, but to check on them. You are not meant to police your partner; give them breathing room and space! Even if your spouse has been disloyal in some way in the past, rather than police him or her, talk about it! Talk about ways to move forward; talk about everything and anything; just talk... only be certain you both understand each other.

Communication is both talking and understanding.

You have built a smooth communication line when you can already determine what your partner is trying to communicate to you before it is verbalized. You know when she is stressed and requires a massage, you know when he is hungry for his favorite dessert, you know when he is disturbed about something, you know when she wants to talk but decides to be quiet instead. This will help us build a strong connection in our relationships. You know, you need a strong connection, or at least a fairly strong one, to be able to communicate with someone else in another location, through your device. But in a relationship, you need communication to build a strong connection.

Communication is not about just talking. It is more than just talking. Understanding is a vital part of communication in relationships. Permit me to quote Jim Keller

"Nothing is as easy as talking but as difficult as communicating," writes Keller. "Some married couples believe that they are doing what is required to do when they speak and tell their spouse what's on their minds. Unfortunately, this is just half the battle, and it's the easier half. The key to effective communication is not speaking, nor is it even just listening, but it is about understanding what your spouse is saying so that you can more effectively respond. Listening is probably the most difficult aspect of communication. It is not merely silent; it is allowing your partner to communicate so that you may understand them better. Many couples listen to be a more effective rebuttal in the conflict or to communicate their position better when it's their turn to talk. I recommend "listening between the lines" as the goal to keep in mind whenever you talk. One of the most important aspects of this concept is the focus. To focus more clearly, couples need to avoid the following distractions: physical, relational, mental, emotional, and spiritual distractions because they can hinder communication and, in some cases, completely destroy it. So, the next time you have a time of communication with your spouse, I would recommend that you do not call it a time to talk, but a time of listening."

Communication is a time to talk, listen, and understand. This will help you make headway in making the right choices together. You will understand what you both want and how the choices you might make can affect that. This will help you grow together. None will be leaving the other behind. You will both move forward in your relationship and in life.

CHAPTER THIRTEEN

I will always be grateful for my husband, Derrick. Through God's grace, love, and forgiveness, we have been able to stay together for over twenty-two years. We have had a lot of obstacles and challenges throughout our marriage and have been able to find ourselves back to each other. In our relationship, we came to the understanding that marriage is about being selfless and continuously putting each other before ourselves. There's a running joke between us in which we are trying to out-give one another, not just in material things but of ourselves, and we encourage other couples to do the same.

Selflessness is the bedrock of God's grace, love, and forgiveness. 2 Corinthians 5:21 says He (Jesus) who knew no sin was made sin for us so that we can be made the righteousness of God in Him. So, you see, God had to put us before Christ, he made him a substitute for us. For God so loved...that He gave...

Loving is giving. You cannot love without giving. God did not give us things, even though He blesses us; He gave us His only begotten! That is, He gave us Himself first. This is the foundation of our loving relationship with the Father, the relationship between Christ and His Church.

We can mirror this in our marriages too; in fact, this was what

Paul admonished the married couples in Ephesus to do:

Selflessness can simply be seen as putting someone before yourself. Note that I did not say 'yourself' but your 'self.' We need to understand what self is before we can then understand what it means to be selfless. Naturally, human being tends to be selfish. Like we saw in the very first blame game; a natural man wants to excuse himself from blame and put it on others. Selflessness is accepting blame even when we are both wrong. Selflessness is a heart that readily forgives even before a wrong is committed. Selflessness is the expression of the love that is shed abroad in our hearts (see Romans 5:8). Selflessness is love in action. What is love in action? A quick reminder of 1 Corinthians 13:4-8.

Love is not arrogant or rude. Love does not insist on its own way. Love endures long and is patient and kind; love is never envious nor boils over with the jealousy, and it is not boastful of vein glory.

Love does not display itself haughtily. It is not proud- arrogant and inflated with pride; it is not rude- unmannerly and does not act unbecomingly. Love (God's Love in us) does not insist on its own rights or its own way, for it is not self-seeking. It is not touchy or fretful or resentful, and it takes no account of the evil done to it (it pays no attention to a suffered wrong).

It does not rejoice at injustice and unrighteousness but rejoices when right and truth prevail. Love bears up under anything, and everything that comes is ever ready to believe the best of every person, its hopes are fadeless under all circumstances, and it endures everything (without weakening).

Love never fails (never fades out or becomes obsolete or comes to an end). As for prophecy (the gift of interpreting the divine will and purpose), it will be fulfilled and pass away; as for tongues, they will be destroyed and cease; as for knowledge, it will pass away (it will lose its value and be superseded by truth).

I love this part –Love bears up under anything, and everything that comes is ever ready to believe the best of every person, its hopes are fadeless under all circumstances, and it endures everything, without weakening. The act of being is selfless, it is the display of the love we have on the inside. If you look at all the characteristics of love, none exalts 'self.' It's all about laying aside self to be better, and to do better. Love believes the best of every person... then how much more about your spouse?! When you believe the best of your spouse, it will not be difficult to give yourself to them.

Selflessness –Self-sacrifice

God loved... that He gave. When we love a cause, we will give ourselves to it. When we love a person, we will give ourselves to him or her. We will give ourselves to anything we love. I usually counsel couples not to lose their spark, that willingness to go the extra mile for each other. When a person gives himself or herself to his or her partner, you will discover that there is nothing that can get her way. He or she will not be selfish with other things; it will become easy to give in the relationship. One would think of his or her partner before anything else. Apart from your relationship, your relationship with God also requires self-sacrifice. If you can leverage on the word of God to learn self-sacrifice, it will help you in your marriage. Fundamentally, we are to give ourselves to God. Then our spouses and importantly, our family as a whole; our life's purpose is very important too –giving ourselves to meet a need or to help others.

I once counseled a young couple. They've only been married for a couple of years but have been together for longer. The issue they wanted to be resolved was the husband's stinginess. He finds it hard to readily let go of his credit card for shopping and other obligation of the house. He will rather wait for the end of the year when malls and outlet stores start rolling out black Friday discounted products before he makes major purchases. The wife felt she was the one doing the giving in the relationship, and felt like she is not getting anything in return from her husband. She felt she could put up with his frugal spirit, but she said she was fed up already.

I first counseled them individually before I performed what I call 'a surgery' on their communication line. They've been talking, but understanding has been lacking. Importantly, the husband needed to adjust; he can be extremely thrify sometimes.

The wife also realized that she had been subtly influenced by some of her friends to put pressure on her husband. They've been in a relationship for years before marriage, and their relationship remained smooth despite his frugal spirit; but all of a sudden, issues started springing forth. While the wife needed to know that selflessness means giving without expecting back in return, the man needed to understand that he cannot be proclaiming love for his wife and not give... to love is to give. You cannot be economical about showing your love. They needed to work towards being better individuals together.

Now, how about giving ourselves to ourselves? Does self-sacrifice mean letting go of our freedom and serving others, while we neglect ourselves? No, it's not... you can always keep your freedom and yet serve others.

The fact that you want to explore your individuality and ambition does not stop you from serving others, and serving others will not rob you of your freedom. We should only channel that freedom to serve God, our family, and as many that can be affected positively by our life.

When I discovered God and when the vigor in my relationship was restored was when I was on my way to self-discovery. When I found my identity in Christ, I could see God in my life and my relationship. So, I started exploring the area I perceived my life would have a meaning and at the same time, kept the fire burning in my marriage. I then discovered how I can serve God and yet affect several lives by doing so.

Today – I am over the marriage ministry at church, I provide marriage bootcamps & retreats. My husband is a big supporter of what I do individually and what we do together. He is very active in helping me with marriage ministry, boot camps, and annual retreats.

CHAPTER FOURTEEN

So many times, in relationships, we give our spouse what we want them to have and not what they need. Big lesson learned in our relationship (Derrick and I). This is why communication is so important in marriage. Our relationship has prepared and equipped us to help others as they journey through marriage —truly understanding marriage as a process and a choice. It's not a sprint or even a relay; it's a long marathon. Getting on the track is completely your choice. Marriage as an institution is a choice, so is who to marry. We also make choices in marriage from time to time; but this time, our choices don't just affect us, they affect our spouse also and every member of the family we build together.

You have your preference, taste, likes, and dislikes as an individual. You can be in a relationship and have someone to go through life together, but the way we respond to life generally will be influenced by our personalities, individually. Let's look at a practical scenario, if you decide on what interior decoration you want for your house, the color you prefer, the furniture, how every piece should be arranged in the house, and so on; you will need to keep your spouse in the loop. Even if one of you is making the sole decision, it is the right of the other person to be kept in the loop. Since you are going to live in that house together, it will be selfish to be comfortable in a house where the other person is not comfortable because of the choices you made. If you prepare a meal for your husband or wife, it is only wise to agree on what choice of food you both would want, since you will be eating it together. You might enjoy a meal, and yet the same meal can result in digestive issues if your partner should eat the same. Now, your individuality and freedom do not stop you from enjoying the meal... however alone. If you have to consider your spouse, you are to put him or her first –selflessness. You can choose a variety of other meals you can both enjoy.

Most times, in marriage, you have to focus on you and know who you are. Even through this process, do not neglect your role in marriage – discover your purpose and your marriage purpose. During the time I chose to go back to school – I did not neglect my marital duties. Marriage for us has not always been a hundred percent; in some cases, it has been 90/10, 80/20, 70/30, 60/40, 50/50, or the other way around. I have learned over time to give a hundred percent even if you feel like your spouse is not giving a hundred percent —now again, that's selflessness. This might seem hard to do; however, I chose to be better. In this case, if things do not work out at least; you can walk away with no regrets.

- How to support and influence each other's choices

This has to be deliberate and should be teamwork; since you will be making choices that affect you and your partner directly. Like every organization that wants to thrive, you need to have a regular board meeting and jointly make decisions that affect the stakeholders. Before any major decision is made, you should both talk about it and make God the center of it. Involving God is very important in making the right choices in life. We involve God in the place of prayer. The choices we make go a long way to make or break a relationship.

Remember the lady who chose her career over her husband. Her husband was supportive throughout the period she was breaking new grounds in her career. He contributed to her progress through her career path, but she was never sensitive to his needs. She made choices to become better as an individual; she got better but at the expense of her marriage.

She neglected her marital responsibility and left a communication loophole; someone else was filling outside. Her husband began to long for companionship, his voice and his needs have been drowned in the choices his wife made. Gradually, things deteriorated until it was too late to work things out. Anyone would want to be in a relationship with someone who will choose them over other things. Otherwise, one feels unwanted, unappreciated, and, worse still, an irrelevant part of the person's life.

Choices are made based on decisions. They don't just happen; there's always a process of thinking things through, a resolution, then a follow-up. If you are not in a relationship, then you can make the decision and go through all the processes, and you will be fine. But if you have invited someone else to be a part of your life, their significance in your decision making must not be underrated.

You must (note the word 'must') carry them along through the process of thinking about what to do or not to do, then you can both agree on a resolution; then, you can both follow up, and it might only affect one of you. So, before you start giving yourself to your work when it becomes demanding, speak with your spouse; work out a plan to keep the vigor in your marriage. Never use making money as an excuse to neglect your partner. The money will never take the place of your spouse, once you allow that void in your marriage, even money cannot fill it. You can always work together as a team, so that jobs don't get in the way of the love and intimacy you share.

• How your choices affect your spouse and other factors in your relationship

One of the wonders of nature I admire is when two fetuses share the same womb and then come out identical. But you will soon realize that these are completely different individuals, who think differently and want things done in their own terms.

They can be seen as identical on the outside, and probably they are always together most of the time, but they are totally different individuals. They can end up going in a different direction in life. However, what has been a greater wonder to me are conjoined twins. These are also different individuals who want different things in life and want to get things done differently. Yet, they have to come to a compromise to live together peaceably.

Marriage has always been joining two different individuals in Holy Matrimony; else, it wouldn't be a marriage. However, this is totally according to the will of two individuals; they choose to be joined together. It's a collective choice, not an individual choice. If only one of them wanted to get married and the other one doesn't, then the marriage cannot be instituted between them, at least not until they both give their consent. It's not as though you've been ultimately conjoined; there are many times the joining doesn't work, and the individuals had to go their separate ways.

However, this book is to help you foresee the dynamics of marriage and relationship; so, you can avoid pitfalls. You can be two different individuals who willingly chose the union, and you can also choose to move forward together for as long as possible. Though your individuality and personality will reflect in your choices, you will be making the decisions together.

This is the point I want to make by pointing our attention to the beautiful gift of two separate individuals forced to live as one – the Siamese twins. Everything one does automatically affects the other. Sometimes, eating might be very difficult that one will have to do the eating, while the other simply gets full if they share the same stomach.

Now, every decision you make directly affects your spouse. You might be doing the eating –probably an academic pursuit or progress in your career– you must see to it that your partner gets filled; that his or her needs are attended to also. For you to move on as one despite being two different individuals, you only need to agree. This is the essence of communication and helping each other along.

CHAPTER FIFTEEN

THE PROVERBS 31 WOMAN AND THE PROVERBS 31 MAN

Proverbs 31:1-31 AMP

THE WORDS of Lemuel king of Massa, which his mother taught him: What, my son? What, son of my womb? What [shall I advise you], son of my vows and dedication to God? Give not your strength to [loose] women, nor your ways to those who and that which ruin and destroy kings. It is not for kings, O Lemuel, it is not for kings to drink wine, or for rulers to desire strong drink, [Eccl. 10:17; Hos. 4:11.] Lest they drink and forget the law and what it decrees, and pervert the justice due any of the afflicted. Give strong drink [as medicine] to him who is ready to pass away, and wine to him in bitter distress of heart. Let him drink and forget his poverty and [seriously] remember his want and misery no more. Open your mouth for the dumb [those unable to speak for themselves], for the rights of all who are left desolate and defenseless; Open your mouth, judge righteously, and administer justice for the poor and needy.

A capable, intelligent, and virtuous woman--who is he who can find her? She is far more precious than jewels, and her value is far above rubies or pearls. The heart of her husband trusts in her

confidently and relies on and believes in her securely so that he has

no lack of [honest] gain or need of [dishonest] spoil. She comforts,

encourages, and does him only good as long as there is life within

her. She seeks out wool and flax and works with willing hands [to

develop it]. She is like the merchant ships loaded with foodstuffs; she

brings her household's food from afar [country]. She rises while it is

yet night and gets [spiritual] food for her household and assigns her

maids their tasks. She considers a [new] field before she buys or

accepts it [expanding prudently and not courting or neglecting her

present duties by assuming other duties]; with her savings [of time

and strength] she plants fruitful vines in her vineyard. [S. of Sol.

8:12.] She girds herself with strength [spiritual, mental, and physical

fitness for her God-given task] and makes her arms strong and firm.

She tastes and sees that she gains from work [with and for God] is

good; her lamp goes not out, but it burns on continually through the

night [of trouble, privation, or sorrow, warning away fear, doubt, and

distrust]. She lays her hands to the spindle, and her hands hold the

distaff. She opens her hand to the poor; yes, she reaches out her filled

hands to the needy [whether in body, mind, or spirit]. She fears not the snow for her family, for all her household are doubly clothed in scarlet. She makes for herself coverlets, cushions, and rugs of tapestry. Her clothing is of linen, pure and fine, and of purple [such as that of which the clothing of the priests and the hallowed cloths of the temple were made].

Her husband is known in the [city's] gates when he sits among the elders of the land. [Prov. 12:4.] She makes fine linen garments and leads others to buy them; she delivers to the merchant's girdles [or sashes that free one up for service]. Strength and dignity are her clothing, and her position is strong and secure; she rejoices over the future [the latter day or time to come, knowing that she and her family are in readiness for it]! She opens her mouth in skillful and godly Wisdom, and on her tongue is the law of kindness [giving counsel and instruction]. She looks well to how things go in her household, and the bread of idleness (gossip, discontent, and self-pity) she will not eat. Her children rise up and call her blessed (happy, fortunate, and to be envied); and her husband boasts of and praises her, [saying], Many daughters have done virtuously, nobly, and well [with the strength of character that is steadfast in goodness], but you excel them all. Charm and grace are deceptive, and beauty is vain [because it is not lasting], but a woman who reverently and worshipfully fears the Lord, she shall be praised! Give her of the fruit of her hands and let her own works praise her in the gates [of the city]!

The thrust of this passage is the deliberate intent to shift the extraneous burdens, which has been placed on the woman in marriage while not considering or demanding commensurate actions and/or response from the man.

The intent of this chapter using the famous Proverbs 31 (often used to describe women of virtue) is to compare the man she is expected to marry and the person he must be...

This might be a long chapter because I'll be taking samples of opinions I see. "We hear a great deal about the Proverbs 31 woman. She's become iconic in Christian circles to the point that her familiarity has bred —if not contempt— at least a sarcastic welcome to many conversations. Sadly, because of this, her full significance is often missed though I, for one, could never be weary of studying her. Much has been said of her many virtues, most of us have made lists of them at one time or another. The Global Study Bible Online calls her "an example of full-scale virtue and wisdom toward which the faithful are willing to be molded."

She's industrious, kind, faithful, wise, diligent, generous, thorough, strong, noble, and creative. Perhaps most significantly, she is all of these things because she "fears the Lord" (Proverbs 31:30).

Is there anything else that enables her to be the woman she is? In all the material I have read about her, in all the sermons I have heard and conversations I have had about her, I have never heard anyone mention the Proverbs 31 Man: her husband.

You've heard, "Behind every great man is a great woman." Isn't the reverse also true? Get a pen, let's do a study on Proverbs 31, and take a few minutes to find the man standing behind this woman. I have previously used the Amplified Bible to explain certain things; now, let's do some comparison using the KJV.

"The heart of her husband trusts in her, and he will have no lack of gain." (v. 11) He's confident in who she is and in her abilities. This isn't lip-service, either—he believes in her from his heart. He's looking for (and finding) the best that is in her and emphasizing that.

"She seeks wool and flax and works with willing hands." (v.13)

There's a lot of services involved in what she does, but she's happy to do it. She doesn't mind working for him—even working hard. She gets up early, she's juggling a lot, and she's willing to do it. Apparently, it does not feel like a thankless job.

That may tell us more about him than almost anything else. "She considers a field and buys it . . ." (v.16) We see from this and also from the many areas of industry in which this woman is engaged that the Proverbs 31 man is neither a control-freak nor a micromanager. She has the freedom and authority to govern her realm, and he doesn't need to be an armchair captain. She develops creativity and productivity because she is supported in these pursuits.

"She opens her hand to the poor and reaches out her hands to the needy." (v. 20)

If I understand this rightly, she's giving both financial help and personal service here. I know exactly what that tells us about this husband. When I want to give to or serve someone, when I talk with my husband about it, his first response is always, "Of course! I never want to stand in the way of anything God wants you to do." Can I just tell you how great that attitude encourages me? Even if my idea was just an impulse of the moment, with a husband like that, you could be sure I'll follow through.

"She is not afraid of snow for her household . . . her clothing is fine linen and purple." (v. 21a, 22b)

Her husband is a good provider. She has what she needs to care for the household. We also see that this woman is cherished. She bothers to dress well and tends to her appearance, and we can infer that this pursuit is encouraged. "Her husband is known in the gates when he sits among the elders of the land." (v. 23)

One of only three direct statements about this man, showing us his good reputation and the freedom, he has to be about his business outside the home. He seems to be active in local government, serving in the community. He is respected and respectable, and he is wise.

"Her children rise up and call her blessed; her husband also praises her; 'Many women have done excellently, but you surpass them all." (v.29)

There's nothing sexist about this man—he notices and affirms the gifts and achievements of women, and most particularly of his own remarkable wife. It is interesting that his praise is direct to her;

she is the recipient of his encouragement. In order to know the full extent of her excellence, it is clear that he notices, acknowledges, and admires all that she is and does. He's not even afraid to compare her to other women (May we note that the only comparison he makes is in her favor!).

One could say, "Naturally her husband admires her, who doesn't, she's accomplishing so much and is so wonderful in every way"–thus making her excellence the cause of his praise. I say this carefully because clearly, the main cause is her fear of the Lord, but I'm just asking–could his praise also be a cause of her excellence?"

Perhaps in our everyday society, which is largely patriarchal, the means employed in interpreting, understanding, and applying such parts of scripture mostly shield the man from much responsibility and puts the woman under more pressure.

Seen from a certain view, the mentions of her husband in Proverbs 31 seems to be in passing and requiring little energy, but at a closer look, we'll realize that it runs a lot deeper.

For a man to handle the weight of virtues and degree of success as possessed by the woman, he must be a man secure in his God and in his own achievements. There is the argument of how a woman shouldn't make more or earn more than her man, so as to prevent insecurity on his part. Any man, who can't handle the heat and weight of glory, isn't deserving of such a woman.

And

It is obvious that the journey of the woman isn't devoid of the man's contribution and support as they're both submitted to God. I'll take some time to explain in detail what each "slight" mention of the woman's husband means to my understanding.

We must remember that the chapter didn't begin with talking about the virtuous woman, it was actually the words of a woman to her son, King Lemuel. So, it is obvious that coming from a woman and a mother, it is an advice best adhered to. Before the picture of the virtuous woman was painted, strict instructions were given by the mother to her son, telling him the things he must shun, the things he was to embrace, and the man and king he must be.

This sets a good foundation for us, telling us that it isn't just any man who deserves a virtuous woman. Just as we see in

2 Corinthians 6:14-16 be ye not unequally yoked together with unbelievers: for what fellowship hath righteousness with

unrighteousness? And what communion hath light with darkness? and what concord hath Christ with Belial? or what part hath he that believeth with an infidel? and what agreement hath the temple of God with idols? for ye is the temple of the living God; as God hath said, I will dwell in them and walk in them; and I will be their God, and they shall be my people.

It would be unwise and a recipe for disaster to find such a woman yoked to whom is best describes as a Son of Belial, and vice versa.

CHAPTER SIXTEEN

WATER YOUR FLOWERS

Show your significant other that you love them. 'Show them'... like we have discussed, you don't let people know you love them if it remains a thought. I mean, you didn't propose to (or reply to the proposal of) your spouse via your thoughts... did you? You must have voiced your thought. Well, it does not end there; it continues throughout the marriage. Now, the next phase is to show them! One of the most important tools in writing any storybook is the ability to show rather than tell. In our relationships, our 'showing' must be corresponding to our 'telling.' That is, when we tell people we love them, we should be able to do things they can see, that is, create time for them, put in more effort, and remind them how much they mean to you even in the smallest ways. Water your flowers, and they will grow!

In the chimpanzee world, there is something called 'grooming.' It is a social, behavioral pattern among chimps. If you see two chimps that are great friends; watch them, they practice grooming. Their friendship probably started on that note. Also, you will see aunties in the family regularly grooming their little nieces and nephews and even other grownups in the family.

Grooming is simply an act of picking at the hair of another chimp. Here, a chimp is enhancing the appearance of another chimp. It's like when your friend comes over and treat you to a pedicure and manicure. So, grooming is a chimpanzee's way of giving a loved one a minor makeover. They can do this several times a day. Chimps can become friends for life if they both groom each other. Need I say it will be courteous for a male chimp to do the same for his lady... and the lady chimp her man? Grooming each other will be grooming their 'relationship.'

If you don't 'groom' your flower, it will die. Grooming a flower means taking good care of it by supplying it with good soil, water, and, if required, pruning it. Else, it will die. Our relationship is our flower; it must not die. Your spouse is your flower; practice grooming them. How do you groom your partner? How do you water your flower? • It starts with voicing your thought

Always let your partner know how much she or he means to you and how much you care about him or her. It is very wrong to assume they know. The issue is not with the fact that they know, but with you admitting that fact. It should not be hard to admit that you love someone if you actually do. If you can't explicitly let your partner know how you feel, you can leave her or him in doubt. It has to come from you! Don't leave the wonderful things you want to say about your spouse as thoughts; it is unfruitful. It becomes productive when those thoughts are voiced.

Let your partner know how you feel about him or her. Let him know how much he means to you; let her know she is loved and treasured. Do not forget to practice "I love you" regularly, and "I am sorry" and "I forgive you" when necessary.

- Actions Speaks Louder than words

You can't tell someone she means the world to you and you can't even afford to 'spoil' her once in a while; You barely remember to pick up a flower and her favorite chocolate on Valentine's Day; You always forget his birthday, but you remember that of your boss because of his recommendation; grooming your spouse rarely tops the list of your priority in a year. It's not enough to say, "I love you," show it! Let your actions speak louder than words.

Take time out from work, daily stress, raising your kids, and other activities that fill your calendar in a year, squeeze in a vacation.

You will need to plan this and make space for it. Take a vacation – just the two of you.

And this should not replace the once in blue moon dates; it doesn't have to be elaborate... it just needs to be private! Take a soft drink and a bag of snacks, just to spend time together; go watch a movie; you can fill in the list –there are hundreds of ways you can show your spouse "I love you," hundreds of ways you can show "I care."

- Watering your flower is a regular process

You don't water your flower the day you planted your flower and forget about it. That water will be used up, and it can't sustain it; you need to replenish it regularly. You have to watch out and be sensitive to the time it will need to be watered again. Taking care of your flower will mean creating time for it, and it's not a one-time thing; it has to be regularly. Grooming among chimps is a social behavior that has spanned centuries. It is an important social behavior. The chimps do it regularly among themselves. Grooming a chimp once cannot sign you off as his friend; you will need to win his trust, and that means more than a onetime grooming.

For instance, taking your spouse out on a date shouldn't be something you did last before you were married. No one waters a flower once and expects it to grow flourishingly. It has to be regular if you want that effect. Many people always make excuses for being busy, yet they schedule their appointments at the beginning of the year and try as much as possible to work within the schedule. When something is important to you, you will make time for it. When it is essential, you will create a schedule that accommodates it as many times as necessary. How essential is taking your bath regularly? Do you regularly brush your teeth? Are you eating regularly? How about sleeping regularly? They are all essentials; they must be done regularly.

Is your relationship important to you? Do you consider your marriage as significant? Then you will create time for your spouse, and you will do so regularly. If your spouse means something worthwhile to you, you will give her or him worthwhile attention.

At the beginning of the year, plan it. Let it be part of your important appointments scheduled for the year. Do you want your spouse to glow? Groom them; do you want your spouse to grow? Water them.

- Wherever you go, water your flowers.

This is in two phases. Some couples don't live together because of work reasons, academics, or the ministry (our work outside of ministry required Derrick to travel). People are serving their country in the military, navy, marine, pilots, doctors without borders, and many more —and we need them! There have to be people volunteering for our security, people helping with medical challenges where it is needed, there have to be people flying our planes and other jobs that require leaving one's family to pursue. We have Christians taking up responsibilities in these areas too.

They will need to leave their partners for a long periods of time to serve their country or to serve humanity.

You can always make plans to water your flower wherever you go! Never close the line of communication. Take advantage of the better means of communicating available to us. Your services might require you being away for a couple of years; Face-time and skype can be a great tool. Also, make sure you are talking via phone... regularly. Despite the distance, you can have flowers delivered; a phone call can take care of that. How about asking a bakery to deliver something nice for his or her birthday? Distance, when necessary, should never stop us from watering our flower. If you should travel, and then you remember your flowers on the balcony, they will die if not watered before you return. What would you do? At least there will be someone who has keys to your apartment that you can ask for some assistance.

CHAPTER SEVENTEEN

Wholeness is something you find within yourself. You will not find this in the people around you, and you will not find it in your job... more importantly, and you will not find it in marriage! Marriage is the coming together of two whole people to establish wholeness together. Is that confusing? No, it's not. Wholeness is discovered individually, and we must all journey towards this discovery individually. It will prevent putting unnecessary pressure or expectation on your spouse. Self-discovery is an individual thing. Others can help (don't get me wrong), but it is your individual journey and discovery. Many try to find wholeness in their spouses, or worse still, in their kids! You will discover that this will lead to putting pressure on the other individual.

In a relationship, for instance, one person can become very dependent and load the other person with expectations.

When you haven't found wholeness as an individual and you are involved with someone, there will be a longing void that should be filled, and you will tend to expect that person to fill it. I once counseled a young man to get a job; he had too much time on his hands and feels his girlfriend is too busy and does not create time for their relationship. Yet she endeavors to spend time with him on weekends. When he started helping out at a local boys and girls club, things got better between them. He got his mind off seeking wholeness from his partner to discovering it on his own. This removed the tension in their relationship and unnecessary expectations from his partner. Also, a father might want to put pressure on his child to achieve certain things, so he could feel fulfilled. But a sense of fulfillment should be an individual pursuit and discovery. The man should achieve fulfillment and allow his child some space to breathe! That child has every right to find fulfillment as an individual; the role of parents is to support. This is how wholeness also works, and your spouse is there to support you, not fill the void. Wholeness is not fulfillment, but it is a journey to fulfillment in itself. Discovering wholeness is like discovering a pathway to purpose and fulfillment. You begin to journey towards fulfillment after you have established wholeness. People sometimes get it wrong; they feel wholeness is fulfillment, but wholeness points us in the direction of fulfillment. It takes a healthy (whole) athlete to run a race in the first place, and then we can talk about winning the race.

Joyce Meyer said, "For years I had low self-esteem, and I did not like myself. I hated my personality, and I hated the way my voice sounded. Somewhere along the line, through the abuse I had endured growing up, I internalized the shame. I was no longer ashamed of what was happening to me—I became ashamed of me. I was hurting and, consequently, was hurting other people.

Did you know that if you don't like yourself, you are never going to like anybody else, and you won't be able to help your spouse like himself or herself? You will spend all your time trying to prove your own value.

Healing first comes by accepting yourself, knowing that where you are today is not where you will end up, and knowing that God is continually perfecting you, too. We all need to accept the unconditional love of God and acknowledge the fact that God doesn't love us because of what we do - but because of who we are."

Discovering wholeness is equivalent to discovering healing as an individual. Sometimes we hurt so badly, we get into a relationship with that emotional distress, and many always expect their spouses to be the ones that will soothe their pain, only to discover that it is a journey they should have embarked on even before going into that relationship. The word 'whole' is common in the four gospels (that is, Matthew, Mark, Luke, and John) books of the Bible. It was used whenever Jesus prayed for an ill person, and the person gets well; the person is said to be made whole. Let's see two instances.

Matthew 9:20-22 KJV

'And behold, a woman, which was diseased with an issue of blood for twelve years, came behind him, and touched the hem of his garment:

For she said within herself, if I may but touch his garment, I shall be whole.

But Jesus turned around, and when he saw her, he said, Daughter, be of good comfort; your faith has made you whole.

And the woman was made whole from that hour. '

Mark 6:56 KJV

'And whithersoever he entered, into villages, or cities, or country, they laid the sick in the streets and besought him that they might touch if it were, but the border of his garment: and as many as touched him were made whole.'

In both instances, the sick was said to be made whole by faith. Faith in what? They all had faith in Jesus and his ability to heal them (or make them whole). Emotional illness can be easily covered, and one can be sick emotionally for several years and yet look okay on the outside. Few people usually seek help to get whole; becoming whole is an individual choice.

I will later share Joyce Meyer's story, and I believe it will inspire you; her husband was really supportive in helping her find wholeness, but she had to make the decision to discover it herself. She gives us a lead on how to find wholeness —we all need to accept the unconditional love of God and acknowledge the fact that God doesn't love us because of what we do - but because of who we are. Amazing! When we discover God's unconditional love, we will discover who we are.

Your spouse can be supportive and helpful, but marriage should be the coming together of two 'whole' people. That is, you should have searched within and drifted towards wholeness as an individual. This will help you define what your marriage should be all about. Only two 'whole' people can work towards establishing wholeness in their marriage.

Only people who have found wholeness individually can establish one in their marriage. The best way to explain this is; if you want to put together a team of two or three people to help you complete a project or to start-up a business. Now, I am certain you will not want half-baked, unprofessional people on your team; you will go for the experts in that field. It is not your responsibility to make them professionals in what they do! Neither is it the role of the team or the business. So, everyone on the team must come on board individually whole (as experts in their fields); to jointly achieve a different kind of completeness. We can see our marriages as a joint partnership between two whole different individuals. Wholeness is found and hence must be searched within one's self, and not in another. It is the sick person that seeks the doctor; the help others can offer to get him or her to the hospital. Those folks that were healed by Jesus in Mark 6:56 will probably need someone to help them to the street (like one of those folks Jesus healed, who was helped by his friends).

If they had stayed back and refused to seek healing, there will be nothing left to do. This is why seeking wholeness has a lot to do with the faith of the seeker. It has to do with the determination and readiness of the one in need of wholeness. You must recognize the fact that you need to find wholeness in yourself as an individual and not in your spouse or any other person.

Marisa Donnelly shared eleven things that happen when you search for wholeness within yourself instead of another person. **This is usually a mistake in many** marriages, which many times results in the individuals going their separate ways. Frustration sets in when wholeness is not forthcoming, and this is because it is sought in the wrong place. You have to look within to find it. So, what effect does the discovering of wholeness in one's self have?

1. You discover that you were always whole, always complete, and never lacking on your own.

    Searching for wholeness within yourself means that you have stopped relying on others to fill you or complete you. Instead of falling into a relationship with a significant other to find meaning, you look for meaning within yourself, within the things you do, within your emotions and perspectives and opinions. And as you do this, you discover that you were never lacking. You never needed someone's love to fill you, as if parts were missing. You have always been, and will always be, completely whole and full on your own.

2. You realize the magnitude of your spirit and the strength within your skin.

Finding your wholeness means realizing how incredibly strong you are. It means resurfacing and taking a breath of fresh air, confident and renewed. It means noticing the way your muscles move, the way your body shifts, the way your spirit brightens an entire room as you walk in. It means acknowledging all that you've pushed through and will continue to push through every single day.

Finding your wholeness means seeing, in a new and beautiful light, how truly astounding you are.

3. You realize what is truly important to you, without outside influence.

In the past, when you searched for wholeness within others or within your relationships, you were continually influenced by what people thought or believed. Though this may have happened unconsciously, your perspectives, and what you placed importance on were shifted and often dictated by the individuals around you. Now that you have focused on your own identity and self-worth, you can seek those answers within yourself.

4. You learn that love is simply within you and that you deserve it, most importantly, from yourself.

It's human, and often natural to search for love in other people, thinking that their affection and attention towards you will fill this void within your heart. But when you stop looking to others for answers and seek them within yourself, you see that love is already and always within you. You see that love is you, in every single part. And you understand that you deserve love—from others yes, but most importantly, from yourself.

5. You place value in the things you believe in and support those things passionately.

When your self-perception shifts, you begin to realize who you truly are and what you're truly interested in. When you realize that you are a whole, complex, and strong person, you begin to put value in your thoughts, your perspectives, and your beliefs. You start to notice what is important to you and what causes you support. And you passionately support those things.

6. You understand what you cannot compromise on, and stand firm in those decisions.

As you learn your values, you learn what you cannot stand for. You learn what causes you can't indulge in under any circumstances. And as you find your identity and wholeness, you accept and own this about yourself, proudly and confidently.

7. You build yourself into a person who is ready for and interested in love as an addition to your world, not an answer.

As you find wholeness within yourself, you learn that love is not something necessary, in the sense that you're supposed to devote your entire life to the pursuit of it. You learn that love does not equal a sense of self or fullness—that fullness comes from within. And most of all, you learn that love is simply beautiful, a powerful addition to your life, not an answer to everything.

8. You find what drives you and spend your time in the selfish pursuit of it.

Once you discover your wholeness, you realize what sets your heart on fire. You realize what you want to pursue, both personally and professionally, and you do so completely and often selfishly. For the first time, your life isn't dictated by a relationship; rather, it's focused on how you can build yourself and your career by doing the things you love. And your relationship(s) encourages and supports your goals instead of distracting you from them.

9. You discover what scares you and learn, on your own, to face those things.

It's natural to want to have someone carry your burdens, to help you square up to your demons, to solve your problems, or help you battle your fears. But when you search for your sense of self, you realize that what makes you truly strong is your ability to do these things alone. That's not to say you can't ask for help because you can and should, but you are now empowered to be more independent and capable; because you are, and always will be.

10. You learn that you are far more resilient than you think.

Realizing who you are and who you are capable of becoming teaches you that you are so incredibly strong and resilient. Seeing what you've already fought through, and how you will continue to find your footing, even when life gives you turbulence, is inspiring. You have and will overcome.

11. You appreciate yourself for the imperfect, complex, and astounding being you are.

Discovering your wholeness means falling in love with yourself. It means seeing, for the first time, how incredible you are. It means taking the time to put yourself first, to pamper yourself, and to celebrate each success. It means building yourself up after you fall and speaking words of love and encouragement to your heart when you're down. It means understanding that you are imperfect, but taking pride in your flaws and failures, as they have created the person you are today.

It means giving yourself the pure, raw love you've been giving everyone else for so long. It means seeing your worth—both body and soul.

Late Dr. Myles Munroe would say people would usually refer to their partners as their 'better halves,' but he said marriage is a union of two individually whole people (paraphrasing). God created Adam whole, and then he made another whole human being (Eve), not to make him whole but to compliment him.

I discovered wholeness in Christ

Becoming whole and complete within myself gave me a sense of wholeness. Only then was I able and ready to be the wife my husband needed in our relationship. I was being who I thought he wanted me to be I felt like a chameleon, in essence changing for the moment and not understanding why I was doing what I was doing.

Eventually, back to my old habits – no real change could take place until I knew who I was. We had to learn and understand that trust is truly important in our relationships. Most importantly, being whole and complete as an individual is important.

I was continuously nagging about almost everything. I didn't quickly realize that my interaction in my past relationships were affecting my marriage. I had certain fears I nursed and was emotionally attached to. I knew I had to be the wife my husband needed, but at some point, I was lost and totally oblivious of how to go about it. I didn't really know exactly if I was doing the right thing or not. I tried not to bring up matters that might suggest that I had trust issues, but I eventually ended up nagging about the situation. Rather than avoid the situation initially, I was supposed to communicate with my husband so we can move on together, but I tried to be who I thought he would want me to be, the good wife.

I will later realize that talking about it and nagging about it are two different things. I felt like a chameleon; I was calm today and complaining about something tomorrow. There was really no issue; I was the one nursing certain insecurity within. I knew I needed to heal, and be the wife God wanted me to be to my husband.

When we discover God's unconditional love, we will discover who we are. When we accept the unconditional love of God and acknowledge the fact that God doesn't love us because of what we do - but because of who we are, it will help us discover wholeness. Wholeness is found in Christ. Just like in the four gospels, everyone who came to Jesus by faith went back whole. Jesus still heals every form of emotional trauma or pain, insecurity, and lack of confidence in marriage. If we take time out to rediscover ourselves in Christ, we will be discovering wholeness as an individual and in our marriages. I started a journey towards discovering wholeness.

I began to get to know who I am in Christ (I am still today and will be tomorrow, this is an unchanging fact). I began to communicate more effectively with my husband, and he was very supportive through it all.

2 Corinthians 5:17 AMP

'Therefore, if any person is [*engrafted*] in Christ (the Messiah) he is a new creation (a new creature altogether); the old [*previous moral and spiritual condition*] has passed away. Behold, the fresh and new has come! '

Look at that! In Christ, who you used to be does not matter anymore; God's love has transformed you totally! You are a new creature! Fresh and new! That is, like a newborn baby, you are coming out fresh and altogether new. However, the word 'therefore' cannot start a sentence; something crucial must have been said prior to that (there was a flow of thought, a message Paul wanted to pass across), so let's see the preceding verses (verses 14-16)

'For the love of Christ controls and urges and impels us, because we are of the opinion and conviction that [*if*] One died for all, then all died;

And He died for all so that all those who live might live no longer to and for themselves, but to and for Him who died and was raised again for their sake.

Consequently, from now on, we estimate and regard no one from a [*purely*] human point of view [*in terms of natural standards of value*]. [*No*] even though we once did estimate Christ from a human viewpoint and as a man, yet now [*we have such knowledge of Him that*] we know Him no longer [*in terms of the flesh*] '

The love of Christ is a solace I found in my trying times, and that became an anchor in my marriage. Derrick and I still so much trust in the love of Christ. This is one of the reasons I decided to let my life be a vessel that will show several people that God's love can change every marriage, and every individual positively and gloriously.

CHAPTER EIGHTEEN

Joshua 18:20 AMP

And the Jordan was its boundary on the east side. This was the inheritance of the sons of Benjamin by their boundaries round about, and according to their families.

In Bible days, boundaries were very important. Even among the tribe of Israel, boundaries were used to separate the inheritance of each tribe when they got to the Promised Land. Even though it was one nation, the citizens regarded boundaries as a very important thing. Lack of respect for another tribe's boundary is trespassing and had consequences. Even though it was one nation, the citizens regarded boundaries as a very important thing. Lack of respect for another tribe's boundary is trespassing and had consequences. Today, boundaries are still very much important. Every country has a boundary with the nearest neighboring country. Today, boundaries are still very much important. Every country has a boundary with the nearest neighboring country.

Otherwise, you could just cross to and from Mexico and the United States without any protocol. Indian and Pakistan used to be one country, divided by different belief systems, which resulted in constant conflict, only resolved when dominantly Hindu nation separated from the dominantly Muslim nation.

Today, there's a somewhat tiny boundary between Indian and Pakistan; it can be easily discarded as unimportant, but the citizens of both nations know how significant the borderline is. Boundaries can be as simple as a stream or as large as a sea, a pathway, or it could be barricaded. However, boundaries are important and common to every nation in the world. Boundaries show you respect my sovereignty as a nation, and it is expected of me to respect yours as well. It is not based on conflict but a mutual understanding.

Every relationship is fostered by mutual consent by the parties involved to respect one another's or each other's boundaries. I have discovered that many people simply go into a relationship without setting boundaries from conception. I made that mistake too.

I didn't see the importance, but as I started discovering wholeness as an individual, I also saw the reason to set boundaries in my marriage. This was why I first dealt extensively with the essence of wholeness in the marriage. After you have discovered yourself in Christ (and your spouse has too), one major step to establish wholeness in your family is to set boundaries.

As I began to get to know who I am in Christ, it allowed me to set boundaries in my marriage and begin to be able to communicate more effectively with my spouse. Setting boundaries is something you must actively and collectively work towards as a couple. Setting boundaries is an important part of your journey to wholeness in your marriage. This is why self-discovery, however self-discovery in Christ Jesus as Christians, is very important. When you find wholeness as an individual, you can then see a need to set boundaries in your marriage. It's a partnership; every healthy establishment must have boundaries.

We don't have to go over the fact that those involved must be professionals or qualified to come on board —that's wholeness. Furthermore, boundaries are defined and acknowledged by all stakeholders.

Clearly, Derrick and I started to understand our roles in our marriage through communication, setting boundaries, and finally beginning to do it God's way. We do not put rules to our marriages, however boundaries. Setting boundaries and putting rules for your marriage are two different things. Many people get it wrong. It's not a superior and subordinate relationship; it's a union of two individuals in partnership, fostered by selfless love and commitment. They both made a choice to be involved in the union. Therefore, it is not a superior dictating out rules to a subordinate; however a joint decision of two whole individuals to set healthy boundaries in their relationship.

There was a man who was angrily complaining to me about his wife. He said that she does not listen to him, and she does as she pleases. So, I set an appointment with both of them.

I discovered, like in many relationships and marriages that communication was lacking. The husband barks out commands, what he wants, and doesn't want. The wife shouts back at him, and she will not allow anyone, not even her husband, to make her do what she does not feel like doing. Clearly, they both want to set boundaries, but they are going about it the wrong way. First, they don't have proper communication that can affect a change, and they don't understand the commitment to one another. Also, none is ready to sacrifice for the other; they both want to have their way. So, we started working on their communication. They started to understand the difference between putting rules – do's and don'ts –and setting healthy boundaries in their marriage. The husband must respect his wife's needs and individuality; the wife must respect her husband's desires and individuality. Individual wants are presented suggestively than in an authoritative tone.

I said when you get involved with someone, it is an invitation for them to invade your space; you are opening up yourself to them. I also said that you might want to keep some things from your partner, but you have allowed them into your life, so you can't put them in the dark as regards to everything that will affect your relationship directly or indirectly, either it's in the past, present or some future plans. They have a right to know. Your weaknesses and frailties have also become non-secret to them; you have welcomed them to know you deeply. So usually, the question is, where does the boundary come in? Where do we set the boundaries? How deeply can my spouse invade my space, my individuality, and privacy?

The essence of boundaries in your relationship or marriage is so that both partners can feel comfortable and maintain their individuality and self-esteem. There are certain things you should admit and let your partner know about –therefore, setting boundaries isn't about keeping secrets or keeping certain things from your partner.

Actually, setting healthy boundaries starts with being completely open, admitting to your partner what your belief, philosophy, and values are; what you want, like and dislike; also, and importantly, what your limits are as an individual. It is unambiguously admitting who you really are to your partner.

Many times, people want others to adjust to what they want as an individual, and other times, people focus on trying to adjust to what others want. What this does is that it shifts the focus of that individual from focusing on himself or herself and what his or her boundaries are to lording over others or trying to please others. Once you are trying to lord what you want and who you are on your partner, that is not setting boundaries; it is putting rules to your relationship. And when you are trying to please your spouse in your relationship, you are most likely the one trying to obey those rules – you will lose who you are and what you want in the shadow of pleasing someone else. Setting boundaries for yourself that reflect who you are and who you ultimately want to be will only enhance setting boundaries with your partner in a relationship.

Our individual boundaries in a relationship are very important and must be respected by both parties. This is why it is not what you simply expect your partner to know, without you communicating it to them. There must be a mutual understanding of what your partner wants, who your partner is, his or her limits, values, dislikes, likes... and vice versa. Until it is communicated and well understood, you are yet to set boundaries. A woman once said to me, "I expect him to know that I do not like that sort of a thing, we've been together for more than ten years!" I told her, "Well, you haven't set boundaries in your relationship for a good ten years." Setting boundaries is an active part of your relationship; never leave it to assumption. You have to sit down with your spouse and talk about it. Remember, good communication includes active listening and appropriate responses, not just talking. You may feel like you know your partner well enough, and you can easily guess what they need without having to talk about it first.

Making assumptions can create a lot of misunderstanding in a relationship —never assume you know how your partner feels. It is always in the best interest of both parties to ask each other (create time to talk about it) rather than assume.

Communicate your thoughts and feelings with your partner. It is important that you are honest about your thoughts and how you feel. Also, respect your partner's point of view and feelings. In discussing boundaries, those two ingredients are essential –honesty and respect. You and your partner can take some time out to gather your thoughts and feelings; however, that should not be an excuse to avoid the discussion. Agree on how long you both will need and when you would want to talk about it. Honesty means you have nothing to hide; you are putting everything on the table. This time, honesty in your discussion has a lot more to do with letting how you actually feel known than keeping something from your spouse. That is, this has to do with your happiness. You are, to be honest about what your boundaries are, don't keep anything back even if you feel it is somewhat ridiculous, let your spouse know, and freely talk about how you feel. Respect comes in when your partner's boundaries are laid on the table.

No matter how ridiculous you feel, it might seem like you are to respect their wishes and not show any form of contempt. If there is anything you are not comfortable with, let your partner know – respect and honesty don't have to clash –rather than say, "this is ridiculous," "how do you expect me to put up with this?" Talk about it! Respectfully communicate your point of view. Respecting your partner's boundaries does not end with the discussion; it actually starts after the discussion. During the discussion, you are to hear your spouse out respectfully; respecting your partner's view comes with the step you take afterward.

Setting boundaries and establishing a healthy one at that is a skill, it will take time. See the day you were open and honest about your individual boundaries, and you agreed on respecting each other's boundaries as the day you had a baby in the family. See it as something you need to nurture and take good care of. It means it won't be smooth all through, but you both have to maintain honesty and respect for one another.

Therefore, communication is a constant in your relationship. You will need it from time to time. It is not just a one-time thing, to adequately establish boundaries in your relationship; you will let it grow with time. This means your partner might still step on your toes before realizing that a boundary had been set (you might be the one who forgot too), give it time, time to adjust, and time to learn how to respect each other's boundaries. Always be open with your partner, groom each other, and practice how not to disrespect each other's boundaries together.

You and your spouse also have to decide to follow through on whatever submissions you make as regards what your individual boundaries are. Setting boundaries is not sitting down to talk about it and hear each other out; it is effective in what you do afterward. You both need to follow it through. If you, as an individual, will not do anything about it, it is an invitation to your spouse also to continue to overstep your boundaries.

Many times, in human relationships, we always look for an exception for ourselves. It is not only important that you do something about what you have discussed (and you don't have to wait for your partner to start, you start!); it is as essential not to make any exceptions. Exceptions to your own boundaries without careful consideration, but based on convenience and exceptions to respecting your spouse's boundaries, must be avoided. There can be relevant exceptions but must be discussed just like the boundaries were discussed. Any addition or subtraction to what you have agreed upon must be reviewed. Once you begin to make exceptions without proper consideration, compromise begins to set in; once there is a compromise, there is a breach of trust, and all the boundaries set becomes irrelevant. You can avoid exceptions and compromises if you and your partner will not only agree to set boundaries but take action immediately. Also, if you will settle in your minds, the fact that you are both growing and can make mistakes. You don't expect your partner to become perfect and start to respect your boundaries exactly the way you want; your spouse should not expect the same of you too.

If mistakes happen, take responsibility for your actions! Neither of you is perfect, give room for some overstepping. Give your relationship a chance to grow gradually, which is natural. Instead of immediately putting blames on your spouse if something went wrong –if there was an overstepping –or just for how you feel; take a step backward and do some meditation. Ask yourself if you have taken appropriate actions to respect your partner's boundaries and remind your partner to do the same, even if he or she forgets. You both have a responsibility to contribute positively to your marriage. In every relationship, especially your marriage, when anything goes wrong, make sure you have questioned your contribution to it before blaming any other person. Remember we looked at the blame game,

Adam never considered his role in doing the wrong thing; instead, he blamed God and his wife for his actions; Eve also could have owned up to her carelessness, rather she blamed the devil instead. So, you see, there's always someone to blame; we must always be ready to take responsibility for our actions. Don't be too quick to put it on your spouse; think about it.

Two important parts of taking action are the commitment to it and respecting each other's boundaries. Staying committed to each other's choices as far as your boundaries are concerned is very important. Remember, in talking about it, and you need to agree on every point made or at least reach a point of the discussion for later. If not, a lack of commitment might surface in later years. Therefore, trash out all you need to trash out; compile all you have agreed on and decide to stay committed to them. Trashing out doesn't mean talking down to your partner's opinion and telling them how ridiculous their choices are... it's a big NO! Trashing out is done together, you respectfully look into what has been discussed (these means do not cut short each other; when one person is speaking, the other person is listening. Wait until all that needs to be said has been said) and then you both can decide which one can stay and which one can't, with reasons. Generally, in life, there is no need for trashing anything, if you've not collected everything that needs to be collected, you might be trashing out your best. So be patient to hear each other out, then honestly and respectfully look into it. Like I said, being respectful doesn't affect your honesty. Honesty is letting your spouse know what you are not comfortable with and how you feel as regards his or her choices. However, you don't have to make your feelings known disrespectfully. You can be honest and yet be courteous in your speech.

Commitment to each other's wishes, staying true to respecting each other's boundaries, will have to stand the test of time. Staying committed doesn't mean things wouldn't go wrong; it only means you won't go wrong. Things go wrong in every relationship, but a strong relationship is that both partners decide not to go wrong but to stick together.

When setting boundaries arise in a relationship, three outcomes are possible: you and your spouse will agree to respect each other's boundaries and gradually take actions to do so; you can both agree to respect each other's boundaries, but the challenge is with taking corresponding actions subsequently; thirdly, there might be no agreement from the start.

In the first category, progress has already been established, so there's no need to talk about that further. Now, the spotlight is on the second and third categories. The second one, you have both agreed on what you both want and do not want, how you expect to be treated and not to, to stay committed to all you have discussed and so on; however, along the way, things are not just working out, it's like you never had the discussion. There's a difference if you are both working at it and recording slight progress, despite some overstepping. But if everything remained as it was before you had the discussion and made the commitment, then there is no progress whatsoever. This can be as a result of the attitude of one of the parties or both of them. Owing to many factors, some people might naturally not have respect for other people's boundaries. We all grew up differently and are from different backgrounds, and I have met people who don't have boundaries and are quite carefree; they might not know how to respect other people's boundaries or see a need for one, hence take it seriously. The only solution is to help them understand and see the need. If you as a partner to this kind of person can get the job done... great! If not, you need to seek professional assistance.

Now, to the third category, the easiest solution is to seek counsel together. Professional help will be very important to resolve the disagreement. The agreement is the bedrock on which you can build commitment to and respect for boundaries. It takes two to tango; you can't build anything without an agreement. Your partner must understand that it is for both of you and for the good of your relationship. This is why I always recommend setting boundaries at the initial stage of a relationship —when things start to get serious between the two of you. It is still very much easy to walk away if things do not work out at that point than when you have invested so much into the relationship. However, if you've been married for a couple of years and you are just getting to know this, it's not too late, I also made the decision late into my marriage – Establishing healthy boundaries in a relationship allows both partners to feel comfortable and develop positive self-esteem. To establish boundaries, you need to be clear with your partner on what your beliefs, values, and limits are, who you are and what you desire.

CHAPTER NINETEEN

Joyce Meyer shared her story. She is a minister I respect so much. She has been married to Dave (like she would call him) for more than fifty years! I definitely have a lot to learn from her. You do too. We will look at what she has to say about 'how to become one' and the 'power of agreement' in a relationship later in this chapter, but I want us to lay a foundation first. The truth is that every relationship, and every marriage wasn't perfect from the start; both partners stayed together to weather their challenges. Everything isn't going to be funky every time, one or both of you can get difficult at times, but marriages don't stand because there are no challenges but because both partners decided to face the problem together.

Jesus said; (Matthew 7:24-27)

"So, everyone who hears these words of mine and acts upon them [*obeying them*] will be like a sensible (prudent, practical, wise) man who built his house upon the rock.

And the rain fell, and the floods came, and the winds blew and beat against that house, yet it did not fall, because it had been founded on the rock.

And everyone who hears these words of mine and does not do them will be like a stupid (foolish) man who built his house upon the sand.

And the rain fell, and the floods came, and the winds blew and beat against the house, and it fell –and great and complete was the fall on it.

In this instance, what words of Jesus do we need to build our homes (marriages) on, that is, act upon them? Living in agreement as we ought, Jesus said, "for this reason, a man shall leave his father and mother and shall be united firmly (joined inseparably) to his wife, and the two shall become one flesh." Jesus taught agreement, and oneness. If you agree with your spouse, no matter how strong the flood or wind might be, you will become an unbeatable team. The rain may be falling heavily from above, and the floods rushing vehemently from below, the wind may be blowing strongly, in every direction; a relationship built on oneness is a rock-solid one, it will not be moved.

Every challenge you face is like a storm, if faced by only one party, it can be overwhelming, but if you would join hands together, you will become an indomitable team. When I saw the movie 'fireproof' some years back and 'war room' more recently, by the same producers, I realized that even if a party starts the fight against the storm against their marriage, the goal is usually to get the other party on board. This is because no matter what the storm is or how impossible the challenge might seem, once both partners are on the same page and not in disagreement, they will come out strong. Amos 3:3 says, "Do two walk together except they agree?" there has to be an agreement if two 'work' and 'walk' together, progressively.

Joyce's testimony (you can check out www.joycemeyersministries.org)

One morning, as I sat in my pajamas praying, the Lord said to me, "Joyce, I really can't do anything else in your life until you do what I have told you to do concerning your husband."

The Lord had been dealing with me because I was having problems being submissive. I had such a strong will and was still caught in my defensive attitude from being abused as a child. I was missing out on the blessings God was eager for me to enjoy.

After praying, I got up and went to take a shower in the new bathroom my husband Dave had just installed off our bedroom.

Since he had not yet put up a towel rack, I laid my towel on the toilet seat and started to step into the shower.

Dave saw what I was doing and asked me, "Why did you put your towel there?" Right away, I could feel my emotions getting stirred up. "What's wrong with putting it there?" I asked in a sarcastic tone. As an engineer, Dave answered with typical mathematical logic. "Well, since we don't have a floor mat yet if you put your towel in front of the shower door when you get out, you won't drip water on the carpet while reaching for it."

"Well, what difference would it make if I did get a little water on the carpet?" I asked in a huff.

Sensing the mood, I was in, Dave just gave up, shrugged his shoulders, and went on his way.

As it turned out, I did what Dave had suggested, but I did it by angrily slamming the towel onto the floor. I did the right thing, but I did it with the wrong attitude.

As I stepped into the shower after throwing my towel on the floor, I was filled with rage. "For crying out loud," I ranted to myself. "I can't even take a shower in peace! Why can't I do anything without somebody trying to tell me what to do?" In my frustration, I went on and on.

Although I was a Christian and had been in ministry, teaching others for some time, I lacked control over my own mind, will, and emotions. It was three full days before I calmed down enough to get over that bath towel incident.

For those three days, I was the noisy gong and clanging cymbal described in 1 Corinthians 13.

Love is the highest form of maturity. It often requires a sacrificial gift. If love doesn't require some sort of sacrifice on our part, we probably don't love the other person at all. If there is no sacrifice in our actions, we are most likely reacting to something nice they did for us, or simply pretending to be kind to gain some control over them. Love is almost always undeserved by the person who receives it.

Our decisions should always have a spouse's interests in mind. Even a mediocre marriage requires sacrifice. It is important to understand that true love gives of itself.

Sacrifice means you are not going to have your way all the time. This means both the husband and wife are called to love each other with unconditional love. There has to be a sacrifice of selfish desires if a couple is going to enjoy a triumphant marriage. As for me, every day when I get up, I choose to have a good marriage. I'm not leaving that one for a chance to decide!

Now let's see 'How to become one' and 'The power of agreement' in marriage:

The three-strand cord is a picture of the power that takes place when two people agree for something in line with God's will for them. As two people become one in agreement with each other, there is a tremendous amount of power.

You can have such fun in your marriage when you begin to agree with each other. Do you know that God did not put you together to be miserable? He didn't put you together to fight, pick on each other, or try and change each other. The Bible says that a woman is to enjoy her husband. (See 1 Peter 3:2)

Think about that. I rarely hear a woman say, "You know what? I really enjoy my husband." And God wants us to enjoy each other. He wants us to have fun together. You need to laugh and have fun together.

How to "Become One"

So how do two people with very different personalities—who don't think alike, who don't feel the same about many different things, who don't even like the same kind of food—become one? We know that it doesn't just happen when you both say, "I do." Becoming one is a process that just takes time.

Many times, the longest part of the process of becoming one is in the mind. Couples are sometimes slow to agree in the way they think about things. How does this process of mental agreement take place? Most marital problems include strife from communication problems, sexual misunderstandings, money issues, different goals, and disagreements about parenting. All of these things get worked out between us within the soul's realm of our union—our minds, wills, and emotions. They don't have as much to do with the spirit or the body as they do with what we think about those areas. We can know spiritually what the right thing to do is, but that doesn't mean we will end up doing it.

The Power of Agreement

The Bible says that we are supposed to be in agreement. My husband, Dave, and I have personalities that are about as opposite as we could get. Yet, God has brought us more and more together so that we are starting to think more alike and want more of the same things every day.

We still have two different personalities, and now we can see that God brought our differences together on purpose. It was not an accident. God knew that each of our strengths and weaknesses would complete the other when we became one. The idea of saying, "Why aren't you like me?" is no longer a question in our hearts. We realize that we need each other to be exactly who God created us to be. We no longer pick on each other's weaknesses. Instead, we partake in our strengths and enjoy one another.

There are no two people who need to get in agreement more than a married couple. God has done so much for Dave and me since we have gotten out of strife and learned to humble ourselves to the point that we don't have to be right all the time. Many wars are started in our homes over unimportant issues that don't matter, such as whether to turn left or right out of the neighborhood when both streets go to the same store. If you want to have power in your marriage and in your prayer life, then you have to get along. You can learn how to "disagree agreeably" without causing strife.

The big question is, how do people who are not of one mind learn to agree? The agreement came when the people involved stopping being selfish. A lot of adults still deal with selfishness. All that selfishness amounts to is, "I want what I want when I want it, and I don't really care what you want because I want what I want." Selfishness is an immature inward focus. If each one of us will learn to voice our wants, but choose what best serves everybody in the family, then we will find peace. The key is to care about what the other person needs, and be willing to humble ourselves and do what we can to meet those needs.

CHAPTER TWENTY

Dr. Myles Munroe answered very crucial questions on the relationship. These are questions we ask sometimes, and they are generally subject matters.

How can I build better relationships?

Can you fulfill your purpose in life and have harmonious, thriving relationships?

Are Males and females really compatible?

What is God's plan for men and women?

How can I make my relationships work?

I will like you to do something practical, let's see the extent to which you can answer the questions above before we look at how Dr. Myles explained different concepts that answered these questions. Kindly get a piece of paper and a pen; write what you sincerely feel the answer to each question should be. At the end of this chapter, you will compare your answers and thoughts to that of Dr. Myles (this was how I truly engaged myself in getting answers to my own personal questions).

Dr. Myles Munroe was more popular than the president of his country, Bahamas, in his lifetime. He wasn't only a successful entrepreneur and leader; he was a minister I respected very much (still do) on the subject of all human relationships and marriage particularly. He was still fulfilling the purpose, and his wife was still by his side, fulfilling his purpose with him when he went to be with the Lord. So, we can learn a great deal from a thread of topics on the relationship, he posted on his blog some years back. We have seen a female minister's (Joyce's) perspective; we can now also consider a male minister's perspective. Though he didn't share any personal story, he did raise very crucial subjects that affect both men and women everywhere in the world. Here, we will see the role of man and that of woman, what is the essence of marriage?

What is the place of a woman in society? Who is a real man? And other important questions answered will help us establish the role and importance of each partner in a relationship.

Some years back, Dr. Myles Munroe opened my eyes to certain facts in relationships and its universality –the characteristics, purpose, and the challenges. First, let's look at 'the problem':

A universal problem

For thousands of years, in nearly every culture and tradition in the world, women have been devalued and therefore mistreated in some way. What accounts for this outlook? Why is this problem so universal? The fact that the devaluing of women is so widespread across the globe points to a cause that goes much deeper than mere culture or tradition.

One of the reasons that the plight of the woman has been such a difficult issue to remedy is that it's not easy to change a man's mind about a woman's place in the world. The idea that this is a man's world is very deeply entrenched. Even though legislation might be passed or public policy might change, you can't easily change a man's mindset. This internalized devaluing of women is the reason why women generally continue to be discounted and exploited in almost every society in the world, regardless of certain social and political advances. In industrial nations as well as developing nations, the plight of the female is still very real. Is it tragic to have to admit this is true in our modern society?

In the neighborhood where I grew up, it was common for me to hear men saying, "Woman, do you know who I am? I'm the one who wears the pants around here!" That statement was supposed to imply who was in charge. These days, both men and women wear pants, so who is that statement talking about now? This spirit of male dominance, this attitude of, "Stay in your place; you have no say in this; you have no contribution to make. You have no sense, anyway," has pervaded our societies for thousands of years, and it is a spirit that still has a hold on many nations.

This prevailing attitude is the reason why the social and political advances of women, which on the surface seem to be victories, can become burdens to women because they are, in reality, only one-sided victories. For example, women can declare that they are equal with men, and society can try to enforce this equality, but the attitudes of men (and also other women) may not necessarily be in agreement with this change in status. This can cause perplexity, stress, and conflict. Thus, much confusion about the role of the woman still exists today.

The Man

Let's go to the beginning: the creation of the male-man. We first need to remember that God creates according to the requirements of His purposes. I want to point out here that since the spirit-man dwells in both male and female, we may refer to the male as a "male-man" and to the female as a "female-man." This will remind us that men and women are both "men." The distinctions between men and women are physical and functional, rather than of their essence.

The purpose of man, the spirit, and the purpose of the male are two different things, although they are related. Male was made to serve the needs of man on earth and to enable him to fulfill his purpose.

Genesis 2 gives us a more detailed explanation of the "formed the male: "The Lord God formed the man from the dust of the ground breathed into his nostrils the breath of life, and the man became a living being" (Gen. 2:7). The male was made first, and there was an interlude of time before the female was made.

There is much we can learn about God's purpose for the male by what the male saw, heard, and learned during this interlude.

Remember that the purpose of something determines its nature, its design, and its features. This means that the nature, design, and qualities of males were decided upon by God and created by him according to what he determined was best for the sake of his purposes.

What is a real man? Imagine that you are watching a television show similar to 'To Tell the Truth.' Several contestants try to convince you that they are the Real Man. You have to guess which one is authentic and which ones are the imposters.

Contestant 1; tells you he is the Real Man because he fills the traditional male role: he supports his family financially while his wife cares for the children and the home. As long as he provides a roof over their heads and food for them to eat, he's fulfilling his duty as a husband and father. This man doesn't consider his wife to be his true equal.

Contestant 2; says he is the Real Man because he has a culturally progressive role: he shares household and childrearing responsibilities with his wife while they both pursue their different careers. He thinks of his wife as his equal.

Contestant 3; explains that he is the Real Man because he has been freed from male stereotypes and has decided to take on the nurturer role of caring for the children and home while his wife goes to work. He considers his wife equal to himself or maybe even better since she has a more compassionate, sensitive nature than he does.

These are some of the images of manhood that are competing for men's acceptance today. Many men feel as if they're being asked to guess what a real man is by determining which "contestant" has the most convincing facial expressions and answers. Yet there seems to be no clear-cut winner. In addition, society keeps mixing and matching these images until men don't know what's expected of them anymore.

They are confused and frustrated as they try to sort through their own expectations for manhood while feeling pressure from the various segments of the society that are promoting these images or an impossible combination of them.

Meanwhile, Hollywood is flooding the society with intriguing icons of masculinity, such as James Bond and Rambo. Even though these images are superheroes rather than real men, it's sometimes hard to escape their allure. It's difficult not to start thinking that a real man should somehow imitate the power and resourcefulness they exhibit.

What is God's purpose for the male? Many men are still wondering why they exist. Yet the Creator of man did not leave us guessing about who the male is supposed to be and what he is designed to do. What we will be looking at is the male's ideal purpose. This is not where we are right now. Yet God's ideal is what we should be moving toward, and by his grace, we will.

The Woman

In the mid-1960s, James Brown came out with a song that exposed the spirit of the age, entitled, "It's a Man's World." The song sold a million copies. (I wonder who bought it) James was singing about an attitude that pervades the nations and culture of the world. That attitude is, in effect, "Even though women are here, this world was made for men. It's designed for males. Women are just filling in where needed. You women stay in your place; this is a man's world."

Does the world belong to men? If so, what place do women hold in it?

One of the most controversial issues of our modern times, a topic that has been debated with much discussion and dissension is the role, position, and rights of the woman. Historically, in nearly every nation and culture, women have been regarded as inferior to men, holding a secondary place in the world. The following are traditional perceptions of women that persist today. Women are considered:

Inferior to men, second-class citizens; objects for sensual gratification alone; weak, and incapable of real strength; lacking in intelligence and therefore having nothing to contribute to society; the personal servants, whose only purpose is to meet the needs of their masters; domestic slaves, to be used as desired; objects to be passed around until finished with, and then discarded; subhuman; deserving of abuse.

Depending on where you live in the world, your past experiences, and whether you are a woman or man, the items on this list might shock you, offend you, be discounted by you, or serve as a painful reminder of what you are currently enduring. If you live in an industrial nation that has seen significant improvements in the status of women and the opportunities open to her, you may not think these negative perceptions of women are relevant to your relationship or the interactions between males and females in your society.

Yet the underlying assumptions behind them persist in every nation because they are not so much influenced by legislative and societal changes as they are by ingrained attitudes in the hearts and minds of men and women. Women are misunderstood and degraded around the world, and it is causing them emotional, physical, and spiritual distress.

CHAPTER TWENTY-ONE

God is the first party

Usually, people would say, you and your spouse are the first and second party, while God is the third party. However, God is the foundation of a healthy union; He is the beginning of all things. Many usually give priority to other things other than God. The truth is, in a relationship bound by love, neither the husband nor the wife assumes the position of the first party, while the other should be the second party. No... a union is established by the joint consent of two individuals –it's a joint partnership! In this case, you are both partners in the agreement. You have become 'one,' so you are on the same 'party.' In essence, there is no third party, to begin with. There is a first-party –the beginning of all things, including the first marriage –and that is God, and then there is the second party – you and your partner –in a partnership.

First-party (Genesis 2:18, 21-22)

Now the Lord God said, it is not good (sufficient, satisfactory) that the man should be alone; I will make him a helper meet (suitable, adapted, complementary) for him.

And the Lord God caused a deep sleep to fall upon Adam, and while he slept, He took one of his ribs or a part of his side and closed up the [*place with*] flesh.

And the rib or part of his side which the Lord God had taken from the man He built up and made into a woman, and He brought her to the man.

Second-party (Genesis 2:23-25)

Then Adam said, this is now the bone of my bones and flesh of my flesh; she shall be called Woman because she was taken out of a man.

Therefore, a man shall leave his father and his mother and shall become united and cleave to his wife, and they shall become one flesh.

And the man and his wife were both naked and were not embarrassed or ashamed in each other's presence.

Many would say, "but the man was made first..." which means he should be the second party as I have explained (or the first party as generally believed), while his wife who came later should be the third party or the second party as the case may be. However, it is important we follow the narrative and understand the context of man's existence and the unveiling of the woman after that. First, let's take a quick look at Jesus' answer when the Pharisees raised a question on marriage and divorce, he said, "have you never read that He who made them from the beginning made them male and female, for this reason, a man shall leave his father and mother and shall be united firmly (joined inseparably) to his wife, and the two shall become one flesh?"

Now, when he said 'have you never read...' we know where he was referring to —that fact was documented in the book of Genesis. Then the question will be, for what reason shall a man leave his parents and cleave to his wife (remember the woman is leaving her parents too and cleaving to her man)? The answer would be because they were made (to be) together in the first place! They were made to complement each other – they were made male and female in the beginning! You can quickly see this in the narrative —the woman was formed from the man! She wasn't a different being created to come and be a help to the man, but she was a part of the man, unveiled to be a helper meet (suitable, adapted, and complementary for him). The man and the woman are invariably one... one bone, and one flesh.

When things got more serious between Derrick and I, everything was just spontaneous, we barely thought of seeking God's face about the matter. He later called me to join him at our frequent place to meet one evening; that was when he popped the question. We did not take time to find out what God's plan was, what His purpose and mindset concerning us was, as regards to being a couple. We did not seek Him to find out if we would be compatible as one. This is very important in every relationship; you can prevent many hiccups and be prepared for others. We must have perceived God has a third party instead of the source of our marriage. When you get into a marriage without seeking God first, when you eventually do later, it will not be to prevent and prepare, but it will become a reaction. It will be as though you have gone into a battle ill equipped, and then you had to retreat to be well equipped. However, you have suffered some attacks before retreating. So instead of reacting to your challenges, you can prevent it instead.

It is quite easy to get anyone to be one's life partner, but it is much more difficult to be partners for life. Venturing into marriage without consideration could be a catastrophe. If a business mogul or even a startup wants to set up a business or invest in any business or organization, he or she will make do the research well enough, looking for reliable considerations before committing into it. Marriage is exactly like that. We don't have to delve into marriage without proper findings, discoveries, and considerations. We can get some information through 'others by counseling', however relying on God will go a long way beyond human capabilities. We will know what to do and how to go about it.

If you have been married for years like most people I counsel, I want you to be certain of one thing, and that is God's grace. It is always available for your equipping. To be ill equipped or well-equipped in marriage is completely your choice; God is always available for your equipping. Seeking Him is for our own benefit. You can still heal even if you are hurting right now, and you can still prevent the future hurts. See Him as your first party and the bedrock of your relationship.

We discover who we really are in God

Throughout our being together for more than twenty-four years, I had to learn who I am in Christ, so I could truly love my husband and be the wife he needed and the wife I wanted to be to him. No real change could take place until I discovered who I really am. There is no other place we can find true meaning in life. In Christ, we can find a mirror that reflects who we really are. Everyone wants to find meaning; everyone wants to find his or her identity. Our identity is found in Christ. I figured out who I really am by reading the word of God, spiritual counseling, and prayer. I read and studied the Bible more often; I engaged in spiritual counseling; I read several books on relationships, marriages, and having a happy home.

The word of God (Hebrews 4:12)

'For the word of God speaks live and is full of power [*making it active, operative, energizing, and effective*]; it is sharper than any two-edged sword, penetrating to the dividing line of the breath of life (soul) and [*the immortal*] spirit, and joints and marrow [*of the deepest parts of our nature*], exposing and sifting and analyzing and judging the very thoughts and purposes of the heart. '

The word of God helped me a great deal. It touched me where I needed most. God knows what we need exactly and has provided the information in His word through His infinite wisdom. He had summarized all human needs from before time and made the documentation of His word available from one age to another.

Sometimes, we are expecting a spooky feeling, a loud, roaring voice from above, but God has already spoken and has been documented. So, what do we do when we go to the word of God? We find out what God has already said concerning that circumstance! There is no unique circumstance as it were; there are only unique personalities going through it.

God's word stands sure yesterday, today, and forever. We can rely on it always; it can be applicable to anyone at any age. It exposes, sifts, analyzes, and judges our intents and purposes and then offers a way out when we approach it with a sincere heart.

Spiritual counseling (Psalms 32:8)

'I [*the Lord*] will instruct you and teach you in the way you should go; I will counsel you with My eye upon you. '

Among the multitude of counselors, you will be wise. Only make sure that they are counselors instructed by God. I stayed in a Christian community, where I had access to counsel from the Lord. I also read different materials that instruct applicably on marriage and building a godly home. I learned wholeness and true fulfillment in all those years.

Prayer (Philippians 4:6)

'Do not fret or have any anxiety about anything, but in every circumstance and in everything, by prayer and petition (definite requests), with thanksgiving, continue to make your wants known to God. '

We are admonished not to complain, not to nag about the situation or be anxious. In whatever circumstance we find ourselves in life, and in our marriages, anxiety will not change anything. We always tell other people about what we are going through except God. We complain and nag about it, but we don't take time out to pray. You should have time to pray, you and your spouse. What happens when you pray? The next verse (verse 7) gives us a lead:

'And God's peace [shall be yours, that tranquil state of a soul assured of its salvation through Christ, and so fearing nothing from God and being content with its earthly lot of whatever sort, that is, that peace] which transcends all understanding shall garrison and mount guard over your hearts and minds in Christ Jesus. '

Did you see that?! You will have true peace after you talk to God about the matter. Take time out and practice this exercise more often. Make plans; schedule it for the month and for the week.

We discover true love in God

It is the love of Christ that controls, urges, and impels us. We will only find true commitment and selflessness in God's demonstration of love towards us. The popular scripture – John 3:16; 'for God so loved the world that He gave His only begotten, that whosoever believes in Him should not perish but have everlasting life'–shows us the length to which *agape* love can go. Romans5 says 'this love has been shed abroad in our hearts by God's Spirit.' This means we have the ability to love selflessly.

If we believe Him for our marriages, our marriages will not suffer but will survive and flourish. Anyone who believes in Christ cannot perish; he is full of God's life. Our marriages will also be full of life when we establish it in God. We will learn what it means to be selfless and stay committed. We will also learn what true forgiveness is.

We discover purpose in God

As a young woman who was still knowing God and discovering purpose, I rested assured and felt that Derrick had an important role to play in my life, along with the fulfillment of purpose. Today, I can confidently say he is such a pillar. He supports me in what I do and a source of encouragement in what we do as a team.

When I started seeking God to rediscover my purpose in life and in my marriage; I started to see myself in the mirror of God's word, I started to see myself in Christ. I was also seeking spiritual counseling at the time. I didn't know what direction I was to take in life, I had finished my University Education at an early age, and I wanted to do better, I wanted to move forward. Yet, my marriage needed some intervention badly, the communication line was almost completely lost, however I was praying to get my man back. Ultimately, I made a decision to go back to college to become a counselor. It was different from what I studied initially, but I perceived that was the direction God wanted me to go in. I finished my master's degree in professional counseling. I attended a Christian University and completed my practicum in a Christian environment; my training allowed me to understand the choice, commitment, forgiveness, and wholeness. This brought light to me as an individual and into my marriage also. I saw the need to pray more and study

God's word more. Not out of necessity, but it had become a part of my life and, consequently, a part of my marriage.

We find purpose in God! Marriage is not a purpose! Rather, marriage gives you a readily available team to help you fulfill the purpose. Do not make the mistake of seeing being married to your sweetheart as an achievement... no! Marriage is to fulfill purpose together. God told the man to be fruitful, to multiply, to dominate and replenish the earth. Even though his teammate was yet to come (yet to be formed, though a part of him), he wasn't lurking around, doing nothing. He was engaging God's wisdom at the time; he was in purpose —he gave names to all the other creatures! So, when the woman came, she met him in purpose.

The man or the wife can have a dream, an idea, a vision that changes the lives of others positively, or that will help others avoid the pitfalls they have encountered and embrace the successes. The wife should always be supportive of her husband in whatever he does; a man stands as a pillar behind his wife such that she is confident in pursuing her life's dream.

Finally, we discover fulfillment in God

No one is truly fulfilled outside God. God is the source of true fulfillment. What is the purpose of our oneness and agreement? When Amos said, "can two walk together except they agree?" it was to what end? They should have a destination that they are heading to. In essence, this is what they agree about. This is because your destination will always determine your route. This is why we find wholeness as individuals and wholeness in our marriages. This is why we need to live in oneness and harness the power of agreement. Remember the tower of Babel, man was united on one sole purpose, and they were going to achieve it. They had a destination, they were determined, and they were all in agreement. If God hadn't stopped them, they would have fulfilled their desire.

I said earlier that you and your spouse are an unstoppable team when you stand together. It's not just that there is no storm you can't withstand together, but there is nothing you can't achieve with the power of agreement. You can fulfill your heart desires as established in God.

CHAPTER TWENTY-TWO

Individual purpose

Most times, in marriage, you have to focus on you and know who you are. Even through this process, do not neglect your role in marriage – find your purpose and your marriage purpose. During the time I chose to go back to school – I did not neglect my marital duties. I knew what direction I wanted to go. It was completely different from what I was doing before, but I knew that was the direction God wanted me to move towards. I decided to go back to college and study as a counselor. I finished my master's degree in professional counseling. Attending a Christian University and completing my practicum in a Christian environment helped me realize how much God wanted me to be whole for myself, for my husband, and for His glory. I started to discover wholeness in every area, and I started to understand the choice, commitment, forgiveness, and wholeness. I just wanted to understand them and apply them to my life, but I then realized that many marriages lacked these things, and many can be prevented from suffering from such deficiencies.

You were born to multiply the gifts and talents that are inside you. There are gifts and talents that God has put inside you. What are you doing to make them grow? If you are a good steward of what has been entrusted to you, then God will reward your faithfulness and entrust you with more. It's a progression of more and more; Jesus called it the kingdom of God. We serve a God who wants to do more in and through you. There is always a thing or another that might come up against our plans, but that would not be enough to make us lose sight of what we are set to do. Accidents or occurrences should rather encourage us to do more and never to give up because we are God's own children! He wants us to live in wholeness, purpose, and fulfillment. God is the source of our dreams. Achieving a purposeful existence is an in-depth desire in every human heart —it is a guiding light from within our hearts. Our life purposes are our guiding light in this world; we will thrive when we discover and walk in them, as an individual and in our marriages.

As a team (purpose in marriage)

You are a team; your ministry together is to help people around you. Remembering you are on the same team is imperative in relationships. When the power of agreement is understood and adequately harnessed, you will see that your partner has an integral part of your team. You can achieve anything you desire as long as it is line with God's plan and purpose for you. It doesn't mean you cannot achieve anything that is not in line with God's plan for your lives. But true happiness and fulfillment are found in staying in God's plan and purpose. If anything goes wrong, if you don't, you will have to bear the consequences together. God's plan will never leave you miserable or unfulfilled. You will be fulfilled as an individual and yet have a fulfilled marriage.

Discovering purpose in God will quickly help you to put others first. There is no selfish purpose in God. Derrick has always been a person who puts other people before himself. He cares very deeply, and I have learned a great deal from him. Our relationship has prepared and equipped us to help others as they journey through marriage. In our boot camps and annual retreats, we have tasked ourselves to consistently encourage spouses who participates in the program. It started as a running joke between us; one person will endeavor to out give the other, not just in material things also in giving of ourselves. We always include this in our workshops as a source of encouragement to others to learn selflessness, giving (because you cannot claim you love and not give and when you are selfless you will want to give) and also, working as a team.

Staying in purpose even as parents

It is a beautiful thing when we are privileged to become parents –it is a beautiful privilege. However, many are quick to forget themselves once they become parents. They forget God's plan and purpose for their own lives, and they become particular about their kids. This can result in putting pressure on your children to fulfill a purpose because you neglected yours. You need to keep focus continually, never set your dream aside, or put your purpose on hold. It is part of your life. If you want to, you can readily raise your children and still fulfill God's plan for you. Having a newborn doesn't mean you should deny yourself all you deserve or desire. Many times, we know exactly what we want to do, how we want to make an impact in our society, but we sometimes become the gremlin that eats up that dream before it materializes at all. We push it away and look for reasons why we cannot. I have discovered that children have always been the excuse of many, especially women.

In today's society, the men see it as their responsibility to take care of their family, so they go all out to get something done. However, carrying the child for nine months, nursing and nurturing is done by the woman. The man can show care and support, but it's the woman who gets the job done. She will need to carry the baby and keep it nurtured inside, go through the delivery and continue the nurturing outside. If only mothers could begin to see that beautiful dream, that vision has another beautiful gift growing on their inside; they will see the need to nurture and protect it. Eventually, there will be a 'safe delivery' of that idea, that dream or vision. Imagine if I had decided to throw away my dream of becoming a counselor, imagine how many people I would have been able to help, but I wouldn't.

Many men also have set aside their life's purpose just to 'feed' the family. I met a man who told me the vision he had been nursing for eighteen years! I asked him why he hasn't pursued it, not even one step. He said the children got in the way; he had to raise a family! He said if it was just him and probably his wife too, he could still risk some things to pursue his dream, but his children still had their future before them; he can't risk some things because of them. I did understand where he was coming from and his plight, but I also understand that this is the excuse we all make. A genuine excuse doesn't transform it from being an excuse, and it's still an excuse.

You should put yourself and your spouse first in some instances. It's not being selfish; it's relevant in God's timeline! We should make sacrifices for our children and extend selflessness to the fruit of our union. Nevertheless, we don't have to take our eyes off our own needs as parents. Our children also need us to be fulfilled in life. What I do has helped me a great deal as a person; it has helped my marriage, but what gives me more joy is the fact that it has helped many others. I don't see it as my dream or vision anymore. It is our dream, our vision; my husband's and mine. He has been there for me from the start. So, as parents, you should realize that before the children comes, you were the ones who were there.

Husbands support your wives, and wives support your husbands. This was what Apostle Paul was telling the Ephesians in essence (see Ephesians 5).

I was elated when I saw an almost ninety-year-old woman dancing so energetically and yet coordinately on one of the popular talents shows. She said she gave up that dream for her family —her husband and kids. However, her husband died early, and when the children were grown, she told them she still had that dream! She

pursued it at that age, and many people around the world watched

her fulfill it. It's never too late to pick up what's left of that vision and

start to put them together.

CHAPTER TWENTY-THREE

Final words

This book is not your typical book on steps on how to stay together. However, this is a way to personally reach out to everyone in a relationship, especially married couples, to share with you how I found purpose and how my husband and I managed to stay together. We have been in a relationship for over twenty-four years, and we've been married for over ten of those years. Derrick and I started out as mutual friends. We went out together on many occasions; we called each other almost every day. It was perfect; I didn't want to commit myself to another relationship because I just got out of one, but I discovered that I began opening up to him more than I would have. I was a quiet person, and I love to keep things to myself and listen to other people tell me stuff about themselves. However, it was different from Derrick, and the feeling was mutual. Soon, it was hard to stay apart, and the climax of it all was when Derrick proposed to me. We were so elated by the years we had spent together, and they are still memories I cherish today.

I shared something crucial in chapter five; God is the bedrock of every healthy relationship. I used the word 'healthy', because it's not perfect, but it is robust and full of life. Other marriages can be positively affected because of yours. Believers ought to take some time out to seek God's face before delving into the big part of life. It is an important part of your life. In many cases, you are probably going to be married for more years than you were unmarried. You will also spend more years being depended upon than the years you spent depending on others. So, you must take your time to seek God's purpose and plan and pursue it.

God told me it wasn't too late to stand strong and stay in His purpose. Though I didn't seek His face at the conception, He was still very much around when I did! He said my marriage can still be as beautiful as I want it to be. He is still saying the same things today. We can still build our relationships on a strong bond of right choices, commitment, love, trust, forgiveness, wholeness, and purpose.

We can still make the right choices that will affect our marriages positively, and we can still have selfless partners who will see themselves as the second party and exalt God as the first. We can still have two whole people living in God's purpose for their lives, helping others find wholeness; we can still have people who will stay committed to each other and respect each other's boundaries, and readily forgiving when there is an overstepping. Yes, we can!

Even though I was a Christian who loved God, however, I didn't initially go about my marriage God's way. Everything didn't work out at some point; I was almost going to give up. At a certain point in our relationship, there was a breach. It certainly was a dark period for both of us. I needed to stand my ground and fight for what's mine. Discovering who I am in Christ was discovering a purpose for me. I wanted my life to be a medium to help other people find wholeness in their marriages. I decided to pursue purpose in marriage counseling, and it is a ministry for me. This was why I decided to send out a message that God's grace, mercy, and forgiveness is richly available for as many that will reach out for it and that faith can be restored to as many who have lost confidence in their marriages; that those marriages can survive and flourish!

'For the love of Christ controls and urges and impels us... Therefore, if any person is [engrafted] in Christ (the Messiah) he is a new creation (a new creature altogether); the old [previous moral *and spiritual condition*] has passed away. Behold, the fresh and new has come! '(1 Corinthians 5:14, 17)

Today – I am over the marriage ministry at our local church, I organize marriage boot camps, workshops, and annual marriage retreats. I also offer counseling services for individuals and couples. My husband is a big supporter of what I do individually and what we do together. He is very active in helping me with the marriage ministry. We stress the point that marriage is a process, and it is forever evolving...

Staying Together